EXTRA

Single Stock Futures:

The Complete Guide

Steven A. Greenberg

Traders Press, Inc.®
PO Box 6206
Greenville, SC 29606

Serving Traders since 1975

Teresa Darty Alligood
Editor and Graphic Designer
Traders Press, Inc.®

Cover Designed by James Roy

Traders Press, Inc.®
PO Box 6206
Greenville, SC 29606

Serving Traders since 1975

Single Stock Futures: The Complete Guide

Table of Contents

To my Mom, for her strength and courage.

To my wife Stacy and our children
Jake, Alex and Charlie
for the joy they bring.

Acknowledgments

I would like to thank my wife Stacy who always appeared interested in hearing about single stock futures. Also for trying to keep the kids busy while I worked on this book. Thanks to my three wonderful boys: Jake, Alex & Charlie (ages 6,4,2) who wanted to help me type and reorganize my research.

To my Father who talked me into this business and my Mother who tried to talk me out of it. If it weren't for the both of them I wouldn't know how to balance my time. I would also like to take this opportunity to thank my Father for continuously providing guidance and support.

Thanks to my partners Barry Isaacson and Carrie Greenberg who were so understanding while I was working on this book.

Thanks to Scott Slutsky for his suggestions and advice, to Dave Meger for his help with the charts and to Nellie Gonzalez for translations. Dan Lazarus and Cheryl Fitzpatrick for guidance with compliance issues. James Roy and his creative abilities with the cover and Lori Greg for keeping everything together.

Thanks to Teresa Alligood for her expertise and patience and Ed Dobson for making working with Traders Press so enjoyable.

Special thanks to Eddie Topple.

Publisher's Comments

For nearly forty years, I have traded in the futures markets. For the first two decades of this period, the vehicles available for trading consisted primarily of agricultural and industrial commodities, and only of tangible items. Later came intangibles, such as currencies and indices. Despite the proliferation of new contracts and markets, the absolute number of markets available in which to trade remained relatively small in comparison with the number of individual equities which offered trading opportunities. But, trading in equities did not offer the advantages of trading in futures, such as the high degree of leverage, ease of entering short sales, lack of complications in transactions such as certificates, dividends, settlement dates, and the like. Now, all that has changed with the introduction of trading in single stock futures. This is a momentous event in the futures industry, which adds many more "markets" to scan for trading opportunities. Being a pattern trader, my method of trade selection involves scanning markets for the patterns that I feel offer significant trading opportunities. Since individual stocks in different sectors often move independently of each other, I anticipate that many additional trading opportunities will be available on a daily basis. Personally, I can't wait to get into the action!

Working with Steven Greenberg, the author of this book and President of *Alaron Trading Company* on the production of this book has been a real pleasure. I am proud that my company, *Traders Press*, is coming out with the first book available on this new and exciting topic. It is our hope that the information in it proves helpful to new and to veteran traders interested in participating in this fascinating new trading vehicle.

Edward Dobson

Edward D. Dobson, President
January 14, 2002
Traders Press, Inc.
Greenville, SC

INTRODUCTION

Definition of Single Stock Futures

Single stock futures are standardized futures contracts on shares of individual companies.

This is truly the beginning of a sea of change in the investment and trading world.

Just as the opening of the Internet to the public created an avalanche of activity in the tech industry, the advent of trading in single stock futures promises to open the doors to unbelievable opportunities for traders, investors, exchanges and brokerage firms alike. This exciting evolution came about through the passage of the Commodity Modernization Act of 2000 that resolved the conflict of jurisdiction over futures on stocks between the Securities Exchange Commission (SEC) and the Commodity Futures Trading Commission (CFTC).

This book will serve as an introduction to the futures markets in general and an authoritative book on single stock futures in particular, including the history of their creation. It is divided into three parts.

Part One gives an overview of the futures and options markets with comparisons to the equities markets.

Part Two is an in-depth look at single stock futures, their trading opportunities and truly unique characteristics.

Part Three details the behind-the-scenes developments that led to the "green light" for the creation of the United States single stock futures markets.

The two most striking differences between trading of single stock futures and equities are the futures trader's ability to leverage his trading capital through more favorable margin requirements (known as performance bonds in futures markets) and the ability to affect a short sale without being encumbered by the short-sale uptick rule of equity markets. These two characteristics alone facilitate an array of arbitrage opportunities between the various options, futures and equities markets.

Individual stock traders are able to hedge their holdings in times of market uncertainties without disturbing their underlying positions. Unlike the stock markets, a single stock futures contract can be sold short without any uptick rule requirement.

Equally appealing is the ability to trade single stock futures electronically. This creates a level playing field in which all participants have immediate access to the market place and corresponding near instant fill reports. Trading costs should be reduced significantly due to the efficiencies of electronic trading platforms.

While untold opportunities exist for the trader trading single stock futures, it is important to remember that with leverage, profit and loss situations can occur rapidly, especially when a company announces good or bad earnings and other corporate actions. Just remember that trading futures is the hardest way to make an easy living. You have to be focused, flexible and disciplined.

Part 1

Futures, Options and Securities

Chapter 1

OVERVIEW

Single Stock Futures

Single stock futures are the latest and most logical derivatives market innovation for the equity oriented trader and investor since the introduction of stock index futures in 1982. Single stock futures allow the individual trader to capture the price movement of the underlying stock, hedge equity positions, and participate in arbitrage opportunities with minimum capital requirements. Trading is on a level playing field where transactions can be effected with a keystroke, with minimum commission costs and with executions reported within seconds. The market will have a high degree of liquidity through registered and regulated exchanges.

As the name implies, single stock futures are futures contracts whose price is derived from the underlying security. Unlike equities, they do not confer ownership rights in the given stock but allow the holder to simply participate in any price movement. In other words, individuals trading single stock futures do not have a voice in shareholder affairs nor receive any dividends. They simply benefit from the price movement of the particular security if in accordance with their position.

One of the most meaningful differences between trading equities and single stock futures is the ability to reverse positions quickly. In equities, one can sell the stock if it is owned but to reverse positions (from long to short) you need what is called an "uptick." Simply put, an "uptick" means that the price at which you sell is higher than the previous sale.

For example, if you wanted to reverse your position on Microsoft (go from long to short), Microsoft would have to trade up from say 56.50 to 56.55 before you would be able to get a short sale off and reverse your position or establish a short one. If you were long the stock, you could sell it without regard to the previous sale and simply be flat. With a single stock future, you could just sell the futures contract on the bid and either be flat (no position) or establish a short position. In other words, futures contracts do not require the onerous "uptick" to establish a short or hedged position. This is a significant advantage because it allows a trader to "go with the flow" and establish a position immediately and not after the majority of the move has occurred or the direction has reversed again.

Another advantage to a person holding an equity position would be the ability to quickly establish a hedge against short-term downward price movements without disturbing the underlying equity position. For example, if one owned Microsoft and wanted to hedge (offset the risk) against an impending announcement, earnings report, or government ruling, they could simply sell a Microsoft single stock future against their stock position. At that time, they would have suspended all price risk and not have disturbed their position in Microsoft. When the trader wanted to lift their hedge, they could buy back the futures contract.

During that period, the price movement would be captured by either the futures contract or the underlying stock position. In other words, each would offset the interim price movement of the other. Say that Microsoft was selling at 56.50 and you sold single stock futures for Microsoft which was selling at 56.60 at that exact time. Whatever amount Microsoft rose or fell during that period would be offset by the Microsoft single stock future which would be moving in near tandem with the equity position. Each would either move up or down by a similar amount, thus offsetting each other.

For those traders equipped with excellent price reporting systems, arbitrage opportunities between the underlying equity and option markets allow the trader with superfast execution systems to capture momentary price inversions between the competing equity and derivative instruments. Arbitrage situations also generate greater liquidity in all of these products. An example of arbitrage, using Microsoft, would be if Microsoft were selling at 56.50 and the futures were selling at 57.00. Tax considerations aside, one could buy the equity and sell the future locking in a gross profit (not including commissions and capital charges) of .50 if held until settlement. Similar situations come up using any combination of options, equities and futures.

Unlike stock index futures, single stock futures will be not be settled in cash. The actual underlying equity is the delivery instrument. Because everyone likes an easy trade, arbitrage opportunities come and go fast but they will be there for the quick, well informed and execution efficient trader.

Unlike equities, futures contracts do not require that the full dollar value of the contract be placed with the executing broker. If Microsoft were selling at 56.50 and one bought 100 shares, you would have to pay your broker $5,650.00 plus commissions. Under current margin rules, you would be required to deposit 50% of the value of the stock plus pay interest on the balance. Using Microsoft single stock futures, you would only have to place a small fraction of the value of the contract (known as a performance bond) with your broker and not have to pay any interest on the remaining fraction. While this feature is very attractive to many traders, it should also be remembered that leverage, as it is called when there is a small down payment, is a two-edged sword. When the futures moves in your direction, the percentage gain vs. capital involved is enormous. However, when there is an adverse movement, it can also result in larger loss as a percentage of capital. Leverage can be a wonderful thing when you are right but can also result in some very quick and large losses as well. Trader beware!

Because most single stock futures are traded on electronic platforms (not open outcry but on an order matching engine like GLOBEX), all participants have the same price information and access to trades as any other. This creates a level playing field because all traders have near instant access to the marketplace without an intermediary. In other words, all traders have "first shot" opportunities at all bids and offers. The first trader to take the offer or hit the bid is the one that gets the trade. No delays or interruptions. Direct access depends on whatever financial arrangements are made with your broker. If the E-mini Standard and Poor's contract is any indication, then electronically traded single stock futures will be awash in liquidity as traders feel comfortable and on the same footing as other market participants.

Efficiencies associated with electronically traded products allow for competitive commission structures because of the reduced costs from not having to staff a trading floor operation that includes telephone clerks, runners, brokers, key punch personnel and others. One great benefit from electronically traded instruments is the time that it takes before you get your trade report. Trade report executions appear on your computer in seconds rather than waiting long, agonizing minutes to hear where your order was filled. And, costs of executions should come down because of electronic order entry efficiencies.

All of the features of single stock futures augur well for their future because they afford the mix necessary for developing liquid markets. Knowing that you have equal access to the order book, knowing that your order reports are fast, knowing that the capital requirements are smaller, knowing that you do not need an "uptick" in the futures contract to reverse your position, knowing all of this gives every trader greater confidence in being involved with single stock futures which has promise to be the greatest trading vehicle since the introduction of stock index futures.

Ban on Single Stock Futures—A Very Brief History of the Shad/Johnson Accord

Knowing all of these wonderful features about single stock futures, one is prompted to ask why it has taken so long for their introduction and acceptance in the United States.

When the green light was given for stock index futures to be traded on futures exchanges in 1982, the idea of single stock futures was also being considered. However, the Commodities Futures Trading Commission (CFTC) and the Securities Exchange Commission became deadlocked as to which one of them would have regulatory authority over this hybrid product of a near-security clone trading on a futures exchange. Rather than have this impasse stall the launch of stock index futures, Congress wisely decided to declare a "moratorium" on single stock futures. The "moratorium" was called the Shad-Johnson Accord after the names of the chairmen of the respective commissions. The moratorium lasted for nearly 19 years until the passage of the Commodities Futures Modernization Act (CFMA) of 2000 signed into law in December 2000.

Why was the "moratorium" on single stock futures lifted as part of the CMA bill? Single stock futures were already being traded in Europe and the fear was that if U.S. exchanges were not allowed to trade them, the marketplace for these products would become embedded on these foreign exchanges. So, it appears that the impetus for lifting the moratorium was not wanting to let the marketplace for these products get rooted on foreign soil. "First mover" advantage was beginning to take place. The London International Financial Futures Exchange (LIFFE) had already listed single stock futures (known over there as Universal Stock Futures) on several leading U.S. companies. Other European exchanges have been trading single stock futures on companies within their own borders for several years already. Trading volume was beginning to build. Once a marketplace for a certain product becomes established, it is hard to dislodge the order flow. Congress, at the prodding of the various futures exchanges, wisely put pressure on the regulatory bodies to resolve the impasse quickly so that product flow would stay on this side of the ocean.

Ironically, synthetic single stock futures could be created all along using options and no government agency seemed to mind. Basically, all one had to do was to buy the same deep in the money call (right to buy) and sell the same (identical price) deep in the money put (right to sell) on any given listed security with listed options and thus create, though somewhat cumbersome, a long futures position that mimicked the price action of the underlying security. To create a short single stock futures position, the opposite options positions had to be taken. Buy the put and sell the call (deep in the money) of the underlying security and you have in effect created a short single stock futures position. Obviously, you would have to make twice the number of transactions in order to achieve the same result offered by trading the real thing but it could have been done though not as efficiently as it is with listed single stock futures. Also, it is trickier to execute such a trade, as the lifting of each option position simultaneously may not be available at favorable bids and offers.

Trading in single stock futures was cleared to begin on August 21, 2001 for certain types of institutional accounts and is tentatively scheduled to begin trading for the retail public in the spring of 2001.

The rules were established in due time so that U.S. did not lose the marketplace for these products to foreign competition operating under the auspices of less bureaucratic structures. Often it can take more than a year to develop deep liquid markets and achieve product acceptance at all levels, both from the public and investment communities of the various financial and fiduciary institutions.

Chapter 2

BASICS OF FUTURES, OPTIONS & SECURITIES

Before one decides to trade single stock futures, they should have a basic knowledge of futures, options and securities markets. This section is not a comprehensive discussion of all aspects of these trading/investment vehicles but a general introduction and an overview of the most visible aspects of these investment instruments.

The Basics of Futures

What is a futures contract? Simply put, futures are about setting future prices. People who trade futures, trade agreements about how much they will buy or sell something for, at a specific date in the future—usually the immediate future, within a few months or less. These agreements are contracts that also specify the quantity and other details of the commodity being traded.

Futures contracts are traded via an auction-like process, with all bids and offers on each contract made public. Through this, a prevailing market price is reached for each contract, based primarily on the laws of supply and demand. This forum is a useful and essential element in a free market economy. You might be surprised to know that the futures markets are rarely used to actually buy or sell the physical commodity or financial instrument being traded; they're used for price discovery, risk management, and of course, investment and speculation.

The futures markets were initially developed to help agricultural producers and consumers manage the price risks they faced with harvesting, marketing and processing annual crops. This type of price determination and risk management has been part of commerce for centuries. The modern futures industry still serves those markets, but has also broadened along with the expansion of our economy beyond its agricultural roots. Today, for example, futures are essential to the financial markets, and provide risk management tools related to currencies, interest rates, securities and stock and commodity .

The futures markets have been successful because they have attracted two kinds of investors/traders: "hedgers" (those seeking to minimize and manage price risk) and "speculators" (those willing to take on risk in the hope of making a profit). The success of the industry is also related to the variety of futures contracts that have been developed to meet the needs of today's extraordinarily complex business enterprises.

Features of Futures Markets

Price Discovery

Far and away, the most important function of a futures exchange is to help centralize the meeting place of buyers and sellers so that all the world can know the current price of whatever is traded. Not having to make numerous inquiries to get a sense of value. It is all established in the floor or in an electronic marketplace at an exchange.

Financial institutions and individual investors alike can look to the futures markets to help determine the best current market prices. That's because the futures market is an independent forum for buyers and sellers who, for whatever reason, want to make a trade. Futures markets provide ways of collecting all the bids and all the offers from around the world and bringing them together. The prices at which these trades are executed determine the best, current market price. In turn, these prices are publicly disseminated, and provide an easy way to determine a product's or instrument's fair price.

Risk Transfer

One of the major functions of modern futures markets is to transfer risk. For example, if you were a farmer or cattle rancher, your objective would be to raise and sell cattle or your crop at a price that would give you the most profit. Your risk would be declining cattle or corn prices. You could transfer this risk by selling cattle or corn futures contracts. If prices plunge, you could buy back the futures contracts at a price lower than you previously sold them. This gain on the futures transaction generally will compensate for your cash loss—hence, the risk of lower prices is transferred. The buyer in this case would be a risk taker—one who thinks that cattle or corn prices are going to rise.

This risk taker can be a speculator or a commercial user (such as a beef processor or cereal manufacturer) who needs the commodity in question and would be adversely affected by higher prices. Those who are willing to accept the transfer of these risks do so in hopes of generating a profit, because they are speculating on whether the price will rise or fall from its current level.

Open Outcry

Most U.S. futures and options contracts are still traded in pits on the floors of futures exchanges via a system known as "open outcry," although a growing number of futures contracts are being traded electronically. Open outcry trading is face-to-face trading, with each trader serving as his own agent. The traders stand in a "pit" (an octagon shaped area with several steps along all the sides) and make bids and offers to one another (via shouting or flashed hand signals) to buy and sell designated contracts.

In most cases, only one type of contract is traded in each pit. For example, there's a Nasdaq 100 pit, an S&P 500 pit, a corn pit, a silver pit and many others. Additionally, each futures exchange trades specific contracts. In some instances, the contracts are licensed or proprietary to the exchange; in other cases, contracts are traded at an exchange primarily because that exchange introduced the contract and developed a group of people who traded it, thus making the contract "liquid."

Liquidity is extremely important as it basically determines whether a market will be viable. Liquidity simply means that there are enough buyers and sellers to make price determination quickly. It is really the gathering of buyers and sellers that makes markets liquid and deep, meaning that you can usually find a buyer or seller for the amount of product that you need at nearly any given price.

It doesn't matter if the bid or offer is made in the "pit" or electronically, the trading process in both cases consists of an "auction" in which all bids and offers on each of the contracts are made known to the public and all participants can see that the market's best price prevails. The word "all participants" is why exchanges are central to creating efficient price discovery.

Electronic Trading

There is a worldwide electronic revolution going on in all financial markets. The traditional "pit trading" is being replaced with electronic exchanges where all bids and offers are matched within a computer server sometimes called a trade matching engine. This revolution began in the early 90's and continues today with whole exchanges being transformed from crowded trading floor arenas to modern, efficient, cost-effective electronic exchanges. In Europe, most of the futures exchanges are entirely electronic and very popular. The nature of exchanges in the U.S. has made this transition more difficult but, nevertheless, there is a shift toward the doing business this way. Most major U.S. futures exchanges offer some of their products electronically. Usually it is for smaller contract sizes of their most popular products. Generally, the products are called e-mini's, "e" for electronic and "mini" for miniature version of the larger contract. When offered electronically, these products have proven to be enormously successful.

Futures Contracts

A futures contract is an obligation to buy or sell a specific quantity and quality of a commodity at a certain price on a specified future date. A futures contract month, also called the "delivery month," identifies the month and year in which the futures contract ceases to exist and when the contract's obligation must be fulfilled. If the contract is not offset (sold if one has bought; bought if one has sold) prior to the delivery date, it is settled either by the exchange of the physical commodity or security, or in cash.

Contract Settlement

The value of a futures contract ultimately is tied to the underlying product or instrument for each contract's specifications. Today, not all contracts are for physical delivery, in which the underlying product is transferred to the futures contract buyer by the seller. A good number are cash settled. Cash settlement allows those who take or make delivery to exchange cash rather than a physical good.

Who Actually Does the Trading?

Most of those who participate in the futures or options markets can be categorized broadly into one of two groups — hedgers and speculators — depending on whether they are there to transfer risk or accept risk. Floor brokers are simply intermediaries who carry out buying and selling instructions from hedgers or speculators.

Hedgers

Hedgers are market participants who want to transfer risk. They can be producers or consumers. A producer hedger wants to transfer the risk that prices will decline by the time a sale is made. A consumer hedger wants to transfer the risk that prices will increase before a purchase is made.

Speculators

Speculators take a position in the futures or options market in the hope of generating a profit. If a speculator takes a long position and the market price goes up, the position is profitable. Likewise, profits accrue on a short position as market prices drop. Similarly if the speculator takes a long position and the market goes down, there will be a loss. Further losses will accrue on a short position as market prices rise.

Locals

An individual speculator who physically trades on the Exchange floor is known as a *local*. Typically, this individual provides market liquidity by constantly buying and selling throughout the trading session. By committing their own trading capital, these traders are willing to assume the risks that others wish to transfer in pursuit of profit.

Buy low/sell high, or vice versa

If you buy something at one price and sell it at a higher price, you make money. If you buy something at one price and sell it at a lower price, you lose money. In futures and options, you can buy and sell in whatever order you want. It's just as easy to "sell high, buy back low," as it is to "buy low, sell high." A contract can be offset at any time during its life by an equal, but opposite, futures transaction to take you out of the market. It's merely a matter of personal choice and perspective as to how long you wish to hold the contract (one hour, or one year). No one way is "best." However, if you hold your position through the contract delivery month, you might have to go through the delivery process. Because most markets can move significantly from one trading day to the next, all participants must pay close attention to current price movements.

Performance Bonds (MARGINS)

The term 'performance bond' or trading on 'margin' in securities means that the investor has borrowed a portion of the funds to buy or sell stocks. The margin requirements in the securities industry are set by the Federal Reserve Band and are currently 50% of the value of the stock purchase or sale with the brokerage firm. Further, the investor must pay interest on the funds borrowed at the margin buyer's interest rate.

Futures exchanges, on the other hand, use the term 'performance bond' or 'margin,' to denote the deposit they require for futures trading. The exchanges set the minimum amount, but each brokerage house can require a greater amount if the markets present excessive risk.

In futures, the total value of the contract is substantially more than the performance bond (margin) deposit. However, margin deposits for securities represent a much higher percentage of the value of the underlying security. No interest is charged for the balance owed on futures contracts. Further, because the performance bond requirements for futures are considerably lower than the actual value of the contract, there are both greater gains and losses as a percentage of the capital deposited. Basically, you have smaller reserve against adverse price moves.

In the case of futures, though you have deposited your 'performance bond,' you should be aware that your liability does not stop there. It is possible to have sudden moves that wipe out the entire performance bond and more. Brokerage firms have risk control departments that stay on top of these situations and alert their customers when they are required to deposit more money. The performance bond is only a deposit and one should be aware that the trader is responsible for all losses should they be greater than the actual initial performance bond.

Marking To The Market

At the end of each trading day and all following days that your position remains open, each contract's value is *"marked-to-the-market."* Your account is credited or debited based on price changes in the underlying futures. This system gives futures trading rock-solid credit standing because losses are not allowed to accumulate.

If your account falls below the maintenance level (a set minimum performance bond per outstanding futures trade), your broker will contact you for additional funds to replenish it to the initial level. Of course, if your position generates a gain, you can withdraw any excess funds from your account.

The Basics of Options

It is important to have a basic grasp of options as they are part of the trading mix that affects the pricing of single stock futures. This section is just an introduction to the basic fundamentals of the options world. There are many complex strategies using options but the information presented here covers the bare essentials. At the end of part three is an important glossary that includes the terminology used in options trading and applies to both the trading of securities, or single stock futures. The vocabulary of the options world in unique and thus it is included in detail after the basic material is presented.

While the discussion here refers to securities, the same elements will apply to options on all futures and single stock futures when they become available in 2003.

What Options Are

An option is a contract that gives the buyer the right, but not the obligation, to buy or sell an underlying asset (a stock or index) at a specific price on or before a certain date (listed options are for 100 shares of the particular underlying asset).

An option, just like a stock or bond, constitutes a binding contract with clearly defined terms and specifications.

In order to better understand options, you should first look at some of the similarities and differences between options and stocks.

Similarities

Listed options are securities, just like stocks. Options trade like stocks, with buyers making bids and sellers making offers.

Options are actively traded in a listed market, just like stocks. They can be bought and sold just like any other security.

Differences

Unlike stocks, options are derivatives (i.e., options derive their value from something else, the underlying security). Options have expiration dates, while stocks do not. There is not a fixed number of options, as there are with stock shares available.

Stock holders own a share of the company, with voting and dividend rights. Options convey no such rights.

There are only two types of options, the call option and the put option.

A **call option** is an option to buy a stock or a futures contract at a specific price on or before a certain date. If you are a buyer, your potential loss is limited to what you pay for the option. That's it.

When you buy a call option, the price you pay for it, is called the **option premium**. Your right to buy that certain stock at a specified price, called the **strike price**, is locked in. If you decide not to use the option to buy the stock, you are not obligated to perform. Your only cost is the option premium.

Put options are options to sell a stock or futures at a specific price on or before a certain date. In this way you know the least that you will get if your position deteriorates in value. You've locked that in and can "sleep" knowing what you maximum risk is.

The primary function of listed options is to allow investors ways to manage risk.

The basic components of the options contract are the premium, the strike price and the expiration date.

An **option premium** is the price of the option. It is the price you pay to purchase the option. For example, a Microsoft May 60 Call (an option to buy Microsoft stock) may have an option premium of $2. This means that this option costs $200.00. Why? Because most listed options are for 100 shares of stock, and all equity option prices are quoted on a per share basis, so they need to be multiplied times 100.

The **strike (or exercise) price** is the price at which the underlying security (in this case Microsoft) can be bought or sold as specified in the option contract.

For example, with the Microsoft May 60 Call, the strike price of 60 means the stock can be bought for $60 per share. Were this the Microsoft May 60 Put, it would allow the holder the right to sell the stock at $60 per share.

The strike price also helps identify whether an option is In-the-Money, At-the-Money, or Out-of-the-Money when compared to the price of the underlying security.

The **expiration date** is the day on which the option is no longer valid and ceases to exist. The expiration date for all listed stock options in the U.S. is the third Friday of the month (except when it falls on a holiday, in which case it is on Thursday). For example, the Microsoft May 60 call option will expire on the third Friday of May.

Exercise of Options

Buyers of options have a right, and that is the right to exercise.

For a **call exercise**, call holders may buy stock at the strike price (from the Call seller).

For a **put exercise**, put holders may sell stock at the strike price (to the Put seller).

Neither call holders nor put holders are obligated to buy or sell; they simply have the rights to do so, and may choose to exercise or not to exercise based upon their own discretion.

This means that when buyers exercise, sellers will be chosen to make good on their obligations.

For a call assignment, call writers (sellers) are required to **sell** stock at the strike price to the call holder (buyer).

For a put assignment, put writers (sellers) are required to **buy** stock at the strike price from the put holder (buyer).

Option Strategies

Now that you are acquainted with the bare essentials of options, we will now delve into the most fundamental strategies using puts and calls. This information applies to whether we are trading options on securities, commodities or single stock futures.

Remember that a call option gives its owner the right, but not the obligation, to buy stock at a certain price and before a certain date and a put option gives its owner the right, but not the obligation, to sell stock at a certain price and before a certain date.

Also, recall that options sellers (writers) are obligated to sell or buy the underlying security, depending if they have sold Calls or Puts, respectively.

When investors open a position by buying Calls, they are **long** those options. When investors open a position by selling Calls, they are **short** those options.

To close the positions, the buyer could sell his long Calls back in the marketplace, and the seller could buy the short Calls back in the marketplace.

The best way to remember the difference between being long or short options positions is to think that you have the right to exercise long options positions and the obligation to fulfill short options positions.

Put Positions are different from Call positions in that the owner has the right to **sell**, not buy, the underlying security. When investors open a position by buying Puts, they are long those options. When investors open a position by selling Puts, they are short those options.

Once again, if you are long options, you have the right to exercise; if you are short options, you have the obligation of assignment.

However, you can always close either position in the marketplace, by simply selling if long and buying back if short.

Let's see how this works.

Long Call Position

Say you bought a call option on Microsoft for $200 ($2 x 100) with a strike price of 60 and at expiration of the option, Microsoft was selling for 67. Your option would be worth $700 and you would have made a $500 profit less execution costs. More than likely, you would have sold the option back into the marketplace (i.e. liquidated the call). Any time before the expiration, you could have sold it as well. Had the price of Microsoft been below 60, you would have let it expire worthless and just been out the $200.

Most options are never exercised but sold back in the marketplace. Index options settle in cash and no action is generally required at expiration because the position is either credited or debited depending on the strike and the settlement price of the underlying instrument. Security options do require performance if exercised.

Long Put, Long Stock

Here's another variation. Say you buy a stock and you are a bit nervous about the short term price movement. You could own the stock but buy a put at a strike price close to the selling price of your stock. Here's an example. You buy Microsoft for 60 and at the same time buy a put with a strike price of 55 for $200. This protects you against any downside price erosion beneath 53. (The strike price less the premium paid.) If the stock continues upward, you simply give up the premium but if the stock drops, you have only two points of risk because you could exercise your put at 55 and be out only the premium plus the 5 point drop in the stock price.

Remember, that the owner of the put has the RIGHT but not the OBLIGATION to exercise. They are in the driver's seat. They are just using PUTS to protect their position.

Long Puts

The last variation is just a speculative usage of put options. One might feel that the price of Microsoft was headed downward and a limited risk way to play that hunch would be to buy a put at a nearby strike price. If the stock indeed did tumble, you could exercise or sell the put for a profit less the execution costs. If you were wrong and the stock soared, your only risk would be the premium paid for the put plus commissions. For example, if Microsoft were selling at 56, you could buy a put with a strike price of $55, say for $100. If the stock fell to 45 while you held the put option, you would gain 10 points less the premium paid of $200, netting $800 less expenses.

Covered Call Writing

When you own the underlying stock and sell a call against it, you are considered a covered call writer. This means that you own the stock and are willing to sell it if the call is exercised. You have downside risk because you own the stock but are willing to assume that risk too. This strategy works best if the stock goes no where. You take in the extra income (the premium) and still own the stock. However, if the stock soars, the call holder will exercise his call. You have to weigh the reward versus the potential for lost opportunity.

These have been examples of very simple options strategies but they are the most basic and most frequently employed.

Exercising Your Options

The owner of an option can exercise that option at any time prior to expiration and conversely a writer (seller) can be assigned any time prior to expiration.

Most options are closed out (sold, or liquidated) in the marketplace. If you are long an option, you sell it back into the marketplace and receive the current bid at that time. If you are short (writer), you pay the going price to close out your position. It is estimated that more than 50 % of all options are closed out in this manner before expiration.

If you decide to exercise a call option, remember that you will become long the underlying security or futures and must have funds available to cover this transaction. If you decide to exercise a put option, you must be able to deliver the underlying security.

The exercise of futures options merely results in the option converting into a futures contract. If you are long a futures call, you become long the underlying futures and if you are short the call, you become short the futures. A put owner who exercise becomes short the futures and the put writer (seller) becomes long the underlying futures.

Stock index futures are settled in cash at the expiration of the contract month as do futures options on these instruments. Single stock futures will be settled in the actual delivery of the underlying security.

How Options are Priced

There are several factors involved in the theoretical pricing of an option. They are:
The price of the underlying stock
The strike price of the option
The time remaining until the option expires
The cost of money (current interest rates less dividends, if any)
The volatility of the underlying security

While the first four factors are known, the aspect of volatility is the least certain it is based on past performance of the stock and is the major determinant for determining the price of an option.

It should be mentioned here that one of the most widely used mathematical formulas used to determine the theoretical value of an options is the Black-Scholes formula. There are others but this one is widely accepted and is "industry standard."

Volatility is important because it "tells" the formula how much to expect the stock price to move in a day, a week or a year. It is also important because it is the only unknown variable in the pricing model. Usually, volatility is based on the stock's historical performance. A change in volatility results in a change in the option's price. It is important to remember that the volatility assigned to a stock is only an educated guess and can change overnight due to many factors. A volatility of 10 on a stock that is trading at 50 means that the stock is likely to trade between 45 and 55. If the volatility doubled, so would the predicted trading range. Volatility ratings can change overnight.

Certain Greek terms are commonly used to describe theoretical pricing described above. Delta is the amount that an option moves in relation to the underlying product. **Vega** refers to the change in option price as it relates to volatility and **theta** is the amount of premium lost each day to time decay.

It is likely that in today's competitive marketplaces, options are fairly priced based upon the above mentioned determinants. The differences in pricing models is really only the estimate of volatility and borrowing costs. All other factors are known.

A few key concepts that need to be understood are:

In-the-money
At-the-money
Out-of-the-money

An **in-the-money option** has a strike price which, for calls, is below the present market price and, for puts, is above the current market price. For instance, if a stock is selling at 55 and you own a call with a strike of 50, the option is 5 points in the money or stated another way, has an intrinsic value of 5 dollars. Any amount in excess of 5 dollars represents the time value of the option. A put would be in-the-money if you owned a put option with a strike of 60 and the stock was selling at 55.

An **out-of-the-money option** has a strike which, for calls, is above the present market price and, for Puts, is below the current market price. For instance, if the stock were selling at 55 and you owned a call with a $60 strike, the option would be 5 points out of the money as there is no intrinsic value. An example of an in-the-money put option would be if you owned a put with a strike of $55 and the stock were selling at $60. The stock would have to fall beneath $55 for the option to have any intrinsic value. Any price available for out-of-the money options can be attributed to the time value portion of the pricing formula. Though an option is out of the money now does not mean that it can't be in the money before it expires and this where the time value comes into play.

An **at-the-money option** has a strike whether Call or Put which is equal to or near equal to the present price of the underlying security. For instance, if you own an option with a $55 strike and the price of the stock is $55, neither a call nor a put has any intrinsic value until the stock moves away from the strike price.

The last factor in pricing is a notion called time decay. This means that as the time length on the option narrows, the premium begins to decrease with a dramatic drop in the last 30 days of the option's life. Each day sees what is called price erosion as the expiration date gets closer. A stock may increase slightly in value but the price of the option may not because the increase (net over intrinsic value) is offset by the time decay.

Volatility changes affect option pricing dramatically. Unfortunately, there is no sure method of predicting future volatility.

If you trust the marketplace to determine efficient options pricing, it really isn't necessary to calculate your own option prices. They will be as close as they can be to what they should be based competitive a competitive marketplace because most market makers use a similar pricing formula and thus tend to keep pricing in line with theoretical values.

This information was just presented for those seeking an understanding of the variables that go into calculating the prices of options. It may be interesting to know but an unnecessary exercise given that an efficient marketplace determines prices for you.

Basics of Securities (Equities)

Issuing stocks allows corporations to raise funds while enabling the investor to make money one of two ways: through the issuance of dividends or through share price appreciation from the sale of profitable shares.

There are two basic types of stocks: common stock and preferred stock. Each type of stock has different characteristics as they apply to the issuance and receipt of dividends, preference of liquidation proceeds, and existence of voting rights.

Stocks can be traded on exchanges like the New York Stock Exchange, NASDAQ, regional stock exchanges, Electronic Communications Networks (ECN's), over the counter dealers, and on the over-the-counter bulletin board.

The United States is the home of the world's biggest and most liquid equities markets which is the reason the world focuses on the U.S. markets in general and that it has been perceived as a safe haven. International commerce is usually transacted in dollars which also adds to the liquidity of these markets.

Common Stock

Common stock differs from preferred stock in several ways.

Common shareholders do not receive a specified dividend.

Common stock may pay dividends, which may vary in amount depending on the company's board of directors. Although common shareholders may receive greater rewards if a company increases in profitability, they are the last to receive payment in the event of a corporate liquidation or dividend payout, after bondholders and preferred shareholders. Additionally, common shareholders are entitled to preemptive rights, stock splits and voting rights.

Preemptive Right

Shareholders of common stock are entitled to what is known as a preemptive right. Preemptive rights occur when a company wishes to issue new stock to the public. However, before the issuance of new stock, common shareholders have the right to purchase new issues in order to maintain their proportional ownership in the company. In the event that preemptive rights are not used, the proportionate ownership in the company would decrease. The shareholder gets a "right of first refusal."

Common shareholders receive one preemptive right per share with further details as to the purchase price (subscription price), issue and expiration date, stated in the rights offering. The owner of common stock preemptive rights may exercise, sell, or transfer their rights to another party.

Stock Splits

A stock split is an increase in a company's number of outstanding shares without any resulting change in shareholders' equity. In the event of a stock split, the total number of shares increases while the corresponding share price decreases. A company may declare a stock split in order to lower the share price to affordable levels and appeal to a larger number of investors.

A reverse stock split is a decrease in the company's number of outstanding shares of stock without any resulting change in shareholders' equity. In the event of a reverse stock split, the total number of shares decreases while the corresponding share price increases. A reverse stock split will typically occur if a company wish to raise its stock price.

Voting Rights

Shareholders of common stock receive voting rights. Voting rights usually refer to the right to vote on major policy decisions as well as general elections for the board of directors. Typically, common shareholders receive one vote per nominee for each corresponding share owned by the shareholder and may engage in a statutory or cumulative voting system depending on the allocation decision of the company.

Classes of Common Stock

A company may elect to classify their stock into designations (such as Class A shares and Class B shares) depending on the requirements as set forth in the corporate charter agreement and bylaws. Generally, Class A shares will possess certain advantages to voting rights, dividend and liquidation privileges over other classes of common stock.

Preferred Stock

Preferred shareholders are entitled to receive dividend pay outs and liquidation proceeds before common shareholders. Shareholders of preferred stock usually receive regular cash dividend payments at a specified rate based on the stock's par value and is usually stated as a percentage of par value. If a company does not maintain a current par value, preferred shareholders will receive a set dividend dollar amount. Additionally, preferred shareholders DO NOT have voting rights.

Cumulative Preferred Stock

Cumulative preferred stock allows shareholders to receive any accumulated back dividend payments in the event the company chooses to omit dividend payments for any period of time.

Convertible Preferred Stock

Convertible preferred stock allows shareholders the option of exchanging their shares for a specified number of common shares.

Dividends

As a shareholder, you are entitled to a portion of the company's distributed profits. Dividends are distributions of earnings, on a per share basis, that are typically issued on common stock in the form of cash or additional stock. If such distribution is in the form of cash, the company will usually issue cash dividends in the form of a check, or they may give the investor the option to reinvest the distribution back into the company through the purchase of additional shares, commonly referred to as a Dividend Reinvestment Plan (DRIP).

Share Price Appreciation

If the investor sells a stock that has increased in value from the original time of purchase, the investor has experienced a share price appreciation. In reviewing share appreciation, it is important to note that there may be little correlation between share price and company performance. More importantly, share prices are affected by the laws of supply and demand, in addition to investor perceptions and expectations of a company's future performance.

Some Factors That Affect The Price Individual Stocks

There are many factors that will determine the price of any given stock. Obviously, in a market system, supply and demand are crucial. But, what affects supply and demand?

Most stocks are earnings driven. If the outlook for a stock and the industry in which it operates is positive, the market places a price on the stock that reflects those earnings. It is called a Price/Earnings ratio. The higher the P/E ratio, the brighter the prospects are for that company and industry.

For instance, XYZ is selling at $56 and earns $4 per share. The P/E ratio would be the price of the stock divided by the earnings. $56/4 or 14 times earnings.

Takeover situations can also drive up the price of the stock.

Other corporate announcements such as earnings forecasts and legal developments may also affect a share's price.

If earnings for a company are on target (meeting analyst's expectations), the company will enjoy the P/E ratio the market has assigned to it. If earnings disappoint analysts, prices can fall dramatically overnight. So, if you own the equity, an option or a single stock futures contract on that stock, the price can swing dramatically up or down on earnings announcements or future prospects of those earnings. Often times stock prices move ahead of earnings reports and already reflect the announced earnings.

Part 2

Single Stock Futures

Chapter 3

TRADING SINGLE STOCK FUTURES

The dawning of a new era in trading products always is met with great expectation and uncertainty that only the marketplace can properly sort out. Such is the case with single stock futures.

Because of the conflict of jurisdiction between the Securities and Exchange Commission and the Commodities Futures Trading Commission, this revolutionary product was delayed from making its debut until 2002. The resolution between these two government agencies was hastened by the fear that a major market for single stock futures would develop overseas before the jurisdictional disputes would be resolved and thus a potentially gigantic market would be lost because of interagency government squabbling. In December 2000 the U.S. Congress signed into law The Commodities Modernization Act of 2000 which, amongst other things, mandated the resolution and legalized the birth of single stock futures.

Before looking directly at single stock futures, it would be very instructive to briefly look at the last big revolution in the trading and investing world, stock index futures and the S&P 500 stock index futures in particular.

Stock index futures began trading in 1982. The idea that an equity index product would be traded on a futures exchange floor and be regulated by the Commodities Futures Trading Commission (CFTC) and not the Securities and Exchange Commission (SEC) was a major victory for the futures industry. However, though single stock futures were discussed at that time as well, the jurisdictional disputes between these two agencies could not be resolved and a "moratorium" on this product was declared. The agreement was known as the Shad-Johnson Accord, and named after the respective agency chairmen.

Initially, the Kansas City Board of Trade developed the Value Line Index, which consisted of 1,700 companies from the New York Stock Exchange, American Stock Exchanges, NASDAQ, and the over-the-counter market. It was an equal-weighted index, meaning that each of the 1,700 stocks is weighted equally. Because liquidity never materialized, the Index languished.

In April of 1982, the Chicago Mercantile Exchange introduced the Standard and Poors 500 stock index futures which consisted of 500 stocks chosen for market size, liquidity, and industry group representation. It is a market-value weighted index (stock price times number of shares outstanding), with each stock's weight in the Index proportionate to its market value.

No one knew how successful these products would be. They were introduced at the bottom of the last bear market and hadn't been tested. As the bull market began to roar in August of 1982, the volume on the S&P's started to climb and continued to do so as hedgers, speculators, money mangers and pension-fund administrators recognized the many opportunities to enhance portfolio return using any number of trading strategies. The market was awash in liquidity and helped attract even more participants world-wide.

Initially the trading hours for the S&P 500 were identical to those of the New York Stock Exchange. Later, they expanded to nearly round-the-clock trading with the introduction of GLOBEX, the electronics trading platform of the Chicago Mercantile Exchange. This change enabled traders around the world to trade daily from their offices, homes, and the exchange trading floors.

The S&P stock index futures allowed traders to play the market as a whole rather than a single stock. It also permitted traders to trade a basket of 500 stocks for a small fraction of the capital requirements had they bought those stocks individually. The leverage here was also very attractive to traders but equally risky when the markets moved opposite their positions. The fact that the S&P's could be shorted without an uptick made this index very attractive to active traders.

Each and every year, trading volume has increased making the S&P 500 stock index futures the most widely watched indicator of stock market activity. It become one of the most successful equity trading products ever launched by an exchange in a short period of time.

So, what does this have to do with single stock futures? A good question. The comparisons are obvious.

Single stock futures are a new product surrounded by a great deal of uncertainty about their acceptance by the marketplace. This was also the case with the S&P 500 Futures initially.

Single stock futures require less capital from the trader than buying stocks on margin. These lower performance bonds, as they are called in the futures industry, allow for greater leverage. Great when you are right but very expensive when you are wrong.

And like the S&P stock index futures contract, the single stock futures contract trader can reverse his position without the uptick rule required on securities exchanges. This feature allows the day trader to capture price moves in either direction because the trader can instantly create a short position rather than waiting for an uptick.

The similarities between stock index futures, which launched nearly 20 years ago, and single stock futures are obvious. The same product features that made the S&P 500 stock index futures contract so successful are also the same ones built into the rules for trading single stock futures. It is reasonable to conclude that all other things being equal, single stock futures will be accepted by the marketplace and enjoy the same success story that their predecessor, the stock index futures did when they were launched in 1982. Stock index futures have paved the way for the birth of single stock futures. You might say they are the parent of this exciting new product.

Now let's look directly at single stock futures and their many, many possibilities for traders and investors alike.

What Exactly Are Single Stock Futures?

As the name implies, a single stock future is a futures contract on a single stock rather than a collection of stocks as in the S&P 500 futures contract, the Russell 2000, and the NASDAQ 100 *et al*. One doesn't have to be concerned with the overall market but rather with the performance of an individual stock.

As it has often been said, it is a market of stocks not a stock market. A stock may be going in one direction while the market as a whole is going in another direction. A single stock future allows the trader/investor to capitalize on the strength or weakness of a particular stock.

Many of the same features of most standardized futures contracts are part of the single stock futures contract design such as unit of trading, delivery months, last day of trading, settlement, minimum price movement, tick value, trading hours and performance bond (margin) requirements. In reality, single stock futures contracts are quite similar to most other futures contracts. The main difference is that the deliverable (bonds, euros, hogs, corn, wheat etc.) is a security rather than a commodity or financial instrument.

Borrowing Stock

To go short means selling a security that you do not own in order to take advantage of an anticipated decline in the price of the security. In order to sell short, the investor must borrow the security from his broker in order to make delivery to the buyer. The short seller will eventually have to buy the security back, or buy to cover, in order to return it to the broker. In thinly traded securities and take-over situations, brokers may have a difficult time locating stock to borrow.

If you wanted to sell your stock on an exchange, you would notify your broker to sell it for you at a given price or at the market, meaning you would accept whatever the highest price bid was for your security when your order arrived at the exchange floor.

However, if you wanted to go short that stock, you would have to wait for an uptick. An **uptick**, simply stated, is a price that is higher than the previous price. For instance, if Microsoft were selling at 59.75 and the previous lower price was 59.70, you could go short the stock at that or at any higher price. However, if it traded back down to 59.70, you would have to wait until it traded at a higher price again. If the stock continued to drop without an uptick for a period of time, you would only be able to get short after the stock had dropped quite a bit and thus potentially miss a major portion of the move. You might be getting short at the bottom of the drop. Certain professional traders under special circumstances are exempt from the uptick requirement but the rules apply to almost everyone else.

The uptick rule was created in the 1930's to prevent "bear market" raids. It was felt that there was something un-American about making money if a stock price went down instead of up. It is an anachronism that will probably be suspended in the near future.

Going Short a Single Stock Futures Contract

Going short a single stock future is an entirely different situation. No uptick is needed. You simply enter a sell order. It's that simple. There's no waiting for the first uptick before you can enter the market. And, you can continue to sell at successively lower bids until your entire position is established. You can go from long to short or just establish a short position with the greatest of ease. Plus, you do so when you want to, not when the market permits as discussed in the rules for going short via the uptick rule.

Most traders are interested in capturing price movement of a stock, whether up or down. The single stock futures contract makes this easier to accomplish because there is no cumbersome uptick rule to accommodate.

When you short a stock, you are attempting to capture the downward price movement. Instead of buying first and selling at a higher price, you sell first and buy later. If you buy at a lower price than you sold it, you've made a profit. It is simply the reverse order of buying first. Either way, your buying price has to be lower than your selling price in order for the trade to be profitable.

For example, you feel that Microsoft will be going down. To short it using the stock itself, you would have to call your broker and tell them to short, lets say, 100 shares at the market. This means that Microsoft would first have to trade at a higher price than the previous best price in order for your order to be executed.

Let's say Microsoft was trading at 58.75 when you entered your order and the previous sale was 59. Microsoft would have to trade higher than 58.75 in order to get your short sale off. Conceivably, it could trade down 3 points before there was an uptick. In other words, Microsoft could trade straight down to

55.75 without an uptick and then trade at 55.80 where you would first be able to enter your short sale.

Now, let's look at going short Microsoft using single stock futures. All you would have to do is instruct your broker to sell a Microsoft single stock futures contract at the market. It would be executed at the first possible moment and would not require an uptick before it could be executed. Using the above prices, your order could be filled at 58.75 while someone trying to go short the actual stock would have to wait until there was an uptick, which could be at a price far away from when they originally entered the order. Single stock futures are the obvious vehicle of choice for short sellers, assuming equal liquidity in both markets.

Liquidity in the single stock futures markets will develop over time and as the orders in the marketplace fill in, the advantage will go to the exchange offering the trader the best and fastest ease of execution.

These two unique features of single stock futures, lower capital requirements and ease of short-sales, are powerful ingredients for making these contracts very attractive to traders.

Margins Versus Performance Bonds

Margin requirements for stocks are set by the Federal Reserve. They are currently 50% of the value of the stock purchase. If you wanted to buy 100 shares of a $100 stock on margin, you would have to put up $5,000 and borrow the balance from your broker at the prevailing margin buyer's interest rate.

In the 1920's, traders were able to buy and sell securities using less than 5% of the value of the security as a deposit. Using only a 5% deposit created excessive speculation. Your leverage factor was 20 times your capital. In other words, a person with $5,000 could control $100,000 worth of stock. That's great if the market moved in the direction of your position but created large and sudden losses when it didn't. It is easy to see that a small adverse move could easily wipe out your deposit. Some think this is what led to the great stock Crash of 1929.

The purpose of the higher margin requirements that followed the Crash of 1929 was to eradicate excessive speculation and prevent another stock market crash of the magnitude of 1929.

Futures exchanges use the term performance bonds to denote the deposit they require for trading futures contracts. Generally, they are set by the exchanges themselves. The performance bonds for single stock futures are higher than they are for almost every other futures contract. However, they are not the same as those used for purchasing stocks on securities exchanges, Even at 20% (pending regulatory approval), of the value of the contract.

Typically, stocks do not move 20% overnight. There is enough time for the firms to ask for additional performance bond deposits if necessary, protecting themselves and the trader as well from adverse price moves.

One can see that the potential return from using single stock futures to capture price movement is greater than trading securities on margin on a listed exchange. There is also the potential for greater losses. Also, unlike securities in which you have three days in which to pay for your purchases, your money must be on deposit with your FCM (Futures Commission Merchant) before you can trade.

Example: A Position In Microsoft

A trader, using margin, buys 100 shares of Microsoft at 60. If he is using margin, he only has to deposit $3,000 with his broker and pay interest on the debit (negative) balance of $3,000. If Microsoft should go up 6 points and he sells, he would have made $600 less commissions, fees and interest. He would have made 20% without consideration of the above costs.

A trader buying a single stock futures contract on Microsoft at 60 and selling out 6 points higher would have made the same $600 less commissions and fees (no interest charges). He would have had to deposit just $1,200 dollars if the performance bond were 20%. Thus, he would have made 50% on his performance bond deposit.

It is easy to see that leveraging makes a dramatic difference.

The above examples show the positive side of leverage. Let's look at the negative side.

In the example where the trader bought stock on margin and was required to put up $3,000 for 100 shares of Microsoft at $60 per share, had the stock fallen 6 points and the trader closed out his position, he would have lost $600 plus the associated costs. As a percentage of his capital deposited, he would have lost more or less 20% of his deposit.

Using a single stock futures contract for Microsoft, the six point loss would have resulted in a 50% reduction in the capital deposited for the performance bond. You can't get away from the fact that where there is greater potential for gain, there is also greater potential for loss. Where there is no potential for gain, there should be no potential for loss.

Single stock futures offer the trader a choice and an opportunity to benefit from leverage. The risks are obvious but the choice is available for the trader. Here's an example of how the price movements of a position in Microsoft would affect your account, performance bond requirements, and maintenance margin requirements.

Day 1: The investor deposited an initial performance bond (margin) of $12,000 with his broker.

The requirements for each of Microsoft single stock futures contract:
Initial performance bond: $1,200
Maintenance margin: $800

Day 2: He bought 10 Microsoft futures contracts @ $60.00. They closed at 61.00 that day and a profit of $1,000 was credited to the account.
$(61.00 - 60.00 \times 100 \times 10 = \$1,000)$

Day 3: Price of Microsoft plunged to 57.50. A loss of $3,500 was incurred for the day. The account balance was still more than the maintenance margin requirement of $800 per contract ($8,000 for 10 contracts).
$(\$61.00 \text{-} 57.50) \times 100 \times 10 = \text{-}\$3,500$

Day 4: Price plunged further to $55.00 A further loss of $2,500 was incurred. The maintenance margin call kicked in, as the account balance was less than the maintenance margin requirement. The investor could do one of the following:
(1) Bring the account back to the Initial Performance Bond level of $12,000 ($1,200 per contract), or
(2) Reduce the number of open position to 6 contracts.

Day 5: He chose to bring back the account to $12,000. No change in settlement price from previous day. The account balance was restored to the minimum performance bond level.

Assumes initial margin of 1200 and maintanence margin of 800. The actual margin requirements had not been determined at time of publication.

Pricing of Single Stock Futures

There is a theoretical value (fair market value) for single stock futures that takes into account the dividend, interest rate and volatility of the underlying security. However, no matter what the theoretical value may be, the marketplace determines the price where that contract trades.

The S&P 500 stock index futures contract often trades at a premium or discount to the "fair market" value. Usually when this occurs, arbitrageur step in and bring the contract back into line by either buying the futures contract and selling the basket of underlying stocks (if the contract is below fair market value) or selling the futures and buying the basket of underlying stocks (if the contract is selling above fair market value).

Since the futures contract cash-settles (is closed out) at a specified date, the contract and the value of the basket of stocks will be identical. Thus, in time, all disparities between fair market value of the contract and the actual value of the underlying basket of stocks disappear.

Though the same pricing considerations for single stock futures will be in play as they are for stock index futures, the actual small size of the contract mitigates a strong interest in arbitrage opportunities. The fair value pricing, the price of the underlying security, and the actual price of the futures contract should be, under most circumstances, fairly close to each other. This would allow only the quickest and most cost-efficient traders to take advantage of temporary market aberrations between the underlying stock and its futures and options derivative companions.

How to Calculate Fair Market Value

Fair market value is the theoretical assumption of where a futures contract should be priced given such things as the current stock price, dividends, days to expiration and interest rates.

The actual futures price will not necessarily trade at the theoretical price, as short term supply and demand will cause price to fluctuate around fair value. Price discrepancies above or below fair value often cause arbitrageurs to return the market closer to its fair value.

Fair Value

The following formula is used to calculate fair value:
= cash [1+r (x/365)] – Dividends
r = interest rate
x = days to expiration

This example shows how to calculate fair value for IBM futures:

Dec IBM futures	93.76
IBM cash price	92.37
Interest rate	2.59%
Dividends to expiration of futures	.14
Days to expiration of Dec futures	25
Fair Value of futures Cash [1 +r (x/365)]-Dividends = 92.37[1+.0259(25/365)]-.14	
Amount of futures overpricing = 93.76-92.37 = 1.399	
Dividend Yield calculation	
IBM dividend yield = .006	
Conversion to Microsoft points	0

FUNDAMENTAL VERSUS TECHNICAL TRADING OF SINGLE STOCK FUTURES

Introduction

There are two major types of analysis for predicting the performance of a company's stock—fundamental and technical. The latter looks for peaks, bottoms, trends, patterns, price, volume and other factors of a stock's price movement. It is a technique many people attempt, though very few are truly successful. Today, the world of technical analysis is huge. There are literally hundreds of different patterns and indicators investors claim to be successful. This discussion covers only the highlights of technical analysis and is not meant to be the definitive work on this subject.

What is Technical Analysis?

Technical analysis is a method that can be used for evaluating single stock futures by analyzing statistics generated by market activity, past prices, and volume. Technical analysts do not attempt to measure a security's intrinsic value, instead looking for patterns and indicators on stock charts that will determine a stock's future performance.

Technical analysis has become popular over the years as more people believe that the historical performance of a stock is a strong indication of future performance. The use of past performance should not come as a big surprise. People using fundamental analysis have always looked at the past performance by comparing fiscal numbers from previous quarters and years to determine future growth. The difference is that a technical analyst believes securities move with predictable trends and patterns. These trends continue until something happens to change the trend, and until this change occurs, price levels are predictable.

Some technical analysts claim they can be extremely accurate a majority of the time. There are many instances of investors successfully trading with only the knowledge of the stock's chart, without understanding what the company does or any of their future objectives. Technical analysis is just another tool, but much more effective when combined with fundamental analysis.

Let's now look at some of the major indicators technical analysts use.

Simple Bar Chart *(MSFT) – Bar charts show data as bars representing High/Low as top and bottom of bar and Open/Close as hash marks on either side of bar (open on the left / close on the right)*

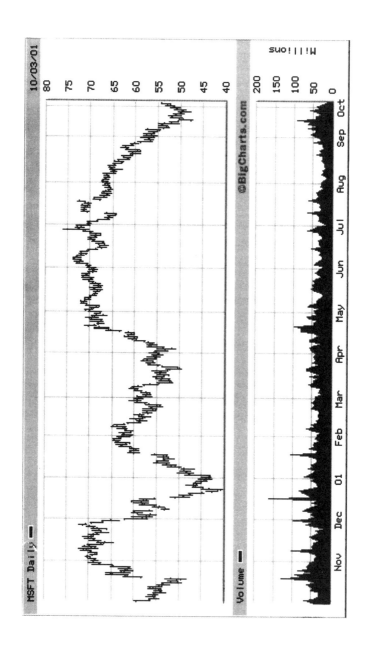

Line Chart (MSFT) – Line charts show data as a continuous line connecting daily closes.

Candlestick Chart (MSFT) – Candlestick chart shows the open, high, low and close (O,H,L,C) data the same as a bar chart; however, the section of the bar between the open and close is shown as shaded or not shaded. The shaded bar represents an open higher than the close (bearish). A bar not shaded represents an open lower than the close (bullish).

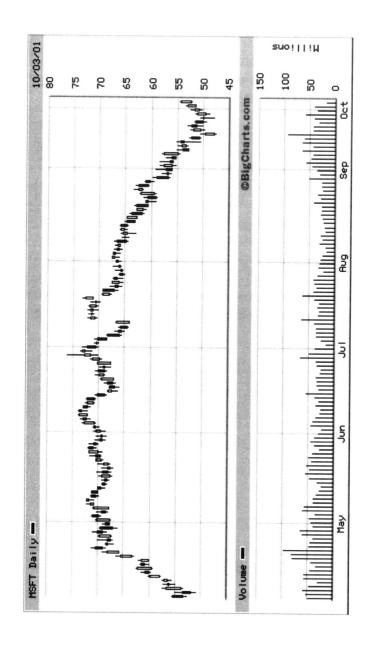

Island Top (MSFT) – Island tops are formed by a small number of trading periods preceded by an upside gap and followed by a downside gap. The formation leaves the period as an "island" on the chart.

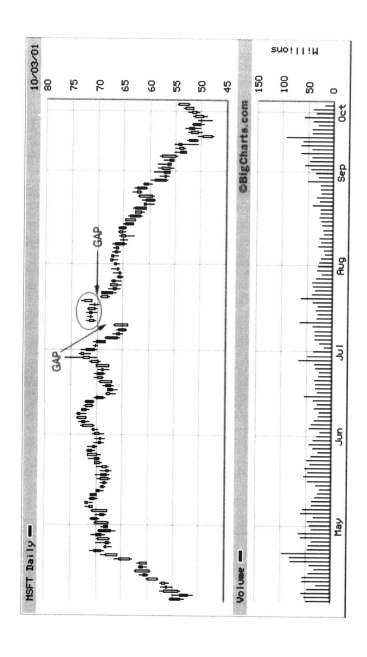

Bullish Candlestick (CSCO) – A bar that is NOT shaded representing an opening at or near the low and a close at or near the high.

Bearish Candlestick (CSCO) – A shaded bar representing an opening at or near the high and a close at or near the low.

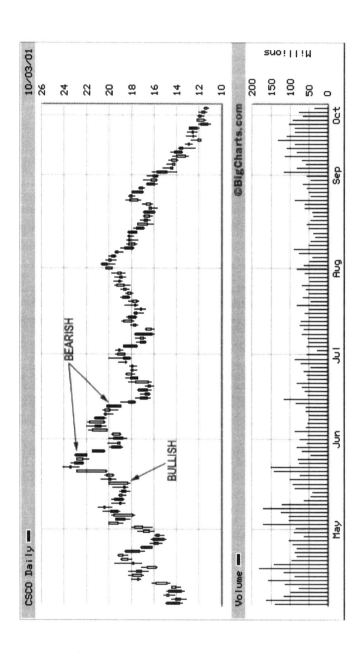

Doji Star Reversal Pattern (CSCO) – Candlestick pattern represented by an open and close of nearly the same price. The open and close of the Doji are normally above the previous and subsequent days' highs and lows.

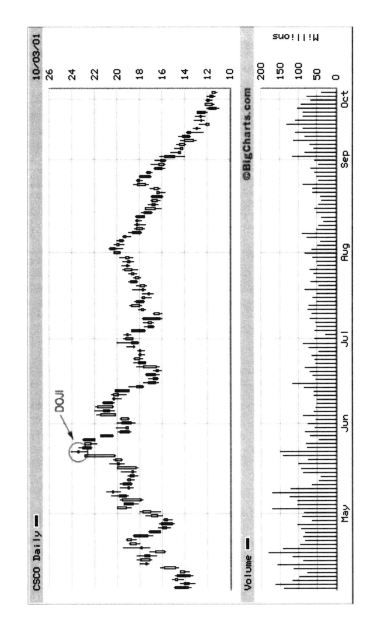

Moving Average (MSFT – showing 9 and 18 day MA) – A technical study representing the average closing for the previous X number of periods (X=9, 9 day moving average). Moving average can be used alone or with another period. A Moving average used alone can trigger a buy or sell with a close above or below the moving average. Two moving averages used together can be used for a buy or sell signal when the moving averages cross. Moving averages are most effective in a trending market and can whipsaw a trader in a sideways market.

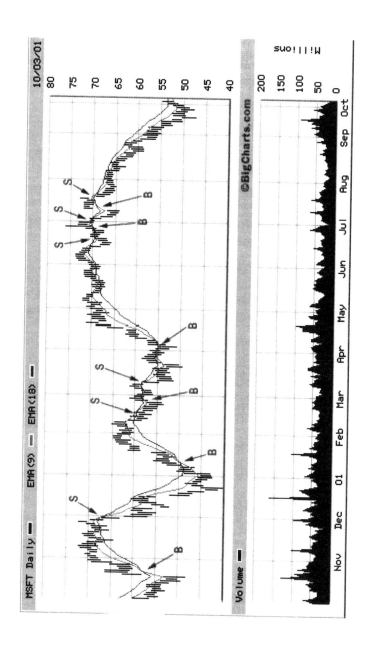

Double Tops and Bottoms (IBM) – Market trades up or down to a previous high or low respectively and is unable to penetrate that price signaling a level of solid resistance or support creating a top or bottom in a market.

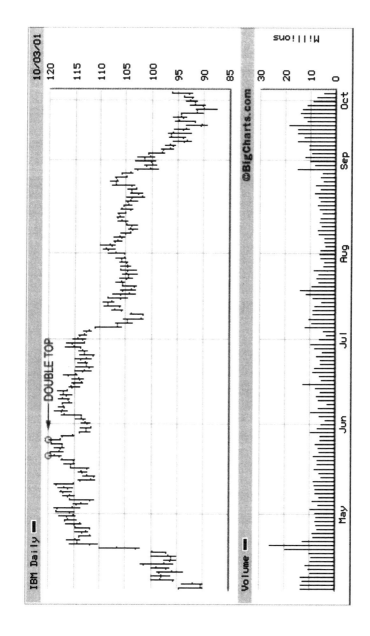

Support and Resistance (MSFT) - Time tested levels of strong buying interest or strong selling interest.

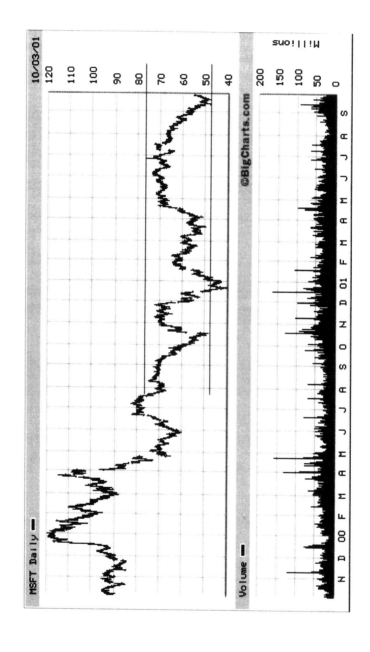

Trend line Support and Resistance (CSCO) - Rising or falling levels of support or resistance creating a trend. Many times trendlines will create "channels" of trading activity.

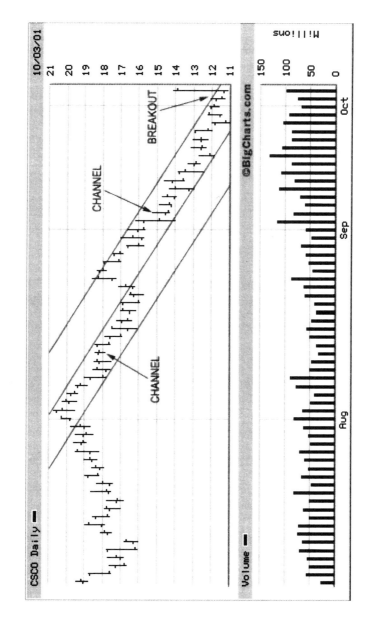

1-2-3 Bottom Formation (MSFT) – A market trades to a low (point 1) and retraces (point 2). The market subsequently falls in an attempt to retest the low, but finds support along the way (point 3). If the market is able to break through point 2 a bottom is formed. The same formation can be used to designate a market top in reverse fashion.

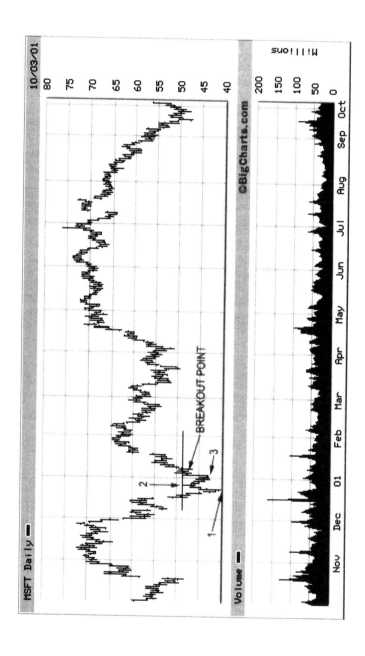

Pennants and Flags (MSFT) – Continuation patterns. Markets have a tendency to return to the current trend after a period of congestion.

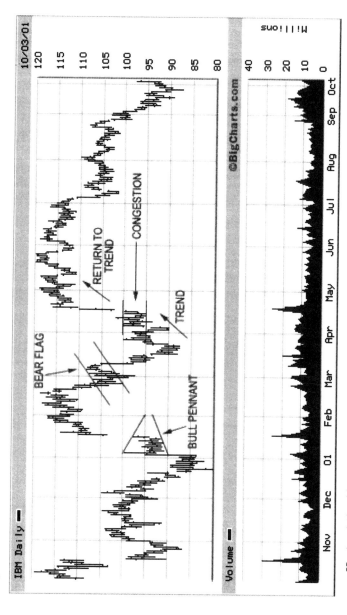

Head and Shoulders Top- A chart formation in which a stock's price:

— rises to a peak and then declines, then
— rises above the former peak and again declines, and then
— rises again but not to the second peak and again declines.

The first and third peaks are shoulders, and the second peak forms the head. This pattern is considered a very bearish indicator.

Head and Shoulders (GM)

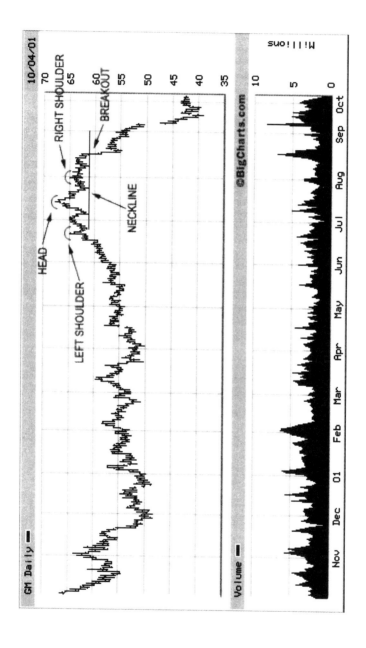

Fundamental Analysis

Fundamental analysis is a method of evaluating securities by attempting to measure their intrinsic value. Fundamental analysts study everything from the overall economy and industry conditions, to the financial condition and management of companies.

In other words, this method uses real data to evaluate a stock's value. It uses revenues, earnings, future growth, return on equity, profit margins, and other criteria to determine a company's underlying value and potential for future growth.

There are many measures that analysts use to determine the financial health of a given company. We will examine the most commonly used indicators.

Fundamental Analysis Overview

Fundamental analysis is the study of economic, industry, and company conditions in an effort to determine the value of a company's stock. Fundamental analysis typically focuses on key statistics in a company's financial statements to determine if the stock price is appropriately valued.

It is quite popular to apply technical analysis to charts of fundamental data, for example, to compare trends in interest rates with changes in security prices. It is also popular to use fundamental analysis to select securities and then use technical analysis to time individual trades.

Interpretation

Most fundamental information focuses on economic, industry, and company statistics. The typical approach to analyzing a company involves four basic steps:

Determine the condition of the general economy.

Determine the condition of the industry.

Determine the condition of the company.

Determine the value of the company's stock.

Economic Analysis

The economy is studied to determine if overall conditions are good for the stock market. Is inflation a concern? Are interest rates likely to rise or fall? Are consumers spending? Is the trade balance favorable? Is the money supply expanding or contracting? These are just some of the questions that the fundamental analyst would ask to determine if economic conditions are right for the stock market.

Industry Analysis

The company's industry obviously influences the outlook for the company. Even the best stocks can post mediocre returns if they are in an industry that is struggling. It is often said that a weak stock in a strong industry is preferable to a strong stock in a weak industry.

Company Analysis

After determining the economic and industry conditions, the company itself is analyzed to determine its financial health. This is usually done by studying the company's financial statements. From these statements a number of useful ratios can be calculated. The ratios fall under five main categories: profitability, price, liquidity, leverage, and efficiency. When performing ratio analysis on a company, the ratios should be compared to other companies within the same or similar industry to get a feel for what is considered "normal." At least one popular ratio from each category is shown below.

Net Profit Margin

A company's net profit margin is a profitability ratio calculated by dividing net income by total sales. This ratio indicates how much profit the company is able to squeeze out of each dollar of sales. For example, a net profit margin of 30%, indicates that $0.30 of every $1.00 in sales is realized in profits.

P/E Ratio

The P/E ratio (i.e., Price/Earnings ratio) is a price ratio calculated by dividing the security's current stock price by the sum of the previous four quarter's earnings per share (EPS).

The P/E Ratio shows how much an investor must pay to "buy" $1 of the company's earnings. For example, if a stock's current price is $20 and the EPS for the last four quarters was $2, the P/E ratio is 10 (i.e., $20 / $2 = 10). This means that you must pay $10 to "buy" $1 of the company's earnings. Of course, investor expectations of company's future performance play a heavy role in determining a company's current P/E ratio.

A common approach is to compare the P/E ratio of companies within the same industry. All else being equal, the company with the lower P/E ratio is the better value.

Book Value Per Share

A company's book value is a price ratio calculated by dividing total net assets (assets minus liabilities) by total shares outstanding. Depending on the accounting methods used and the age of the assets, book value can be helpful in determining if a security is overpriced or underpriced. If a security is selling at a price far below book value, it may be an indication that the security is underpriced.

Current Ratio

A company's current ratio is a liquidity ratio calculated by dividing current assets by current liabilities. This measures the company's ability to meet current debt obligations. The higher the ratio the more liquid the company is. For example, a current ratio of 3.0 means that the company's current assets, if liquidated, would be sufficient to pay the company's current liabilities three times over.

Debt Ratio

A company's debt ratio is a leverage ratio calculated by dividing total liabilities by total assets. This ratio measures the extent to which total assets have been financed with debt. For example, a debt ratio of 40% indicates that 40% of the company's assets have been financed with borrowed funds. Debt can work two ways. During times of economic stress or rising interest rates, companies with a high debt ratio can experience financial problems. However, during good times, debt can enhance profitability by financing growth at a lower cost.

Inventory Turnover

A company's inventory turnover is an efficiency ratio calculated by dividing cost of goods sold by the inventory. It reflects how effectively the company manages its inventory by showing the number of times per year inventory is turned over (replaced). Of course, this type of ratio is highly dependent on the industry. A grocery store chain will have a much higher turnover than a commercial refrigerator manufacturer. As stated previously, it is important to compare ratios with other companies in the same industry.

Stock Price Valuation

After determining the condition and outlook of the economy, the industry, and the company, the fundamental analyst is prepared to determine if the company's stock is overvalued, undervalued, or fairly valued.

Several valuation models have been developed to help determine the value of a stock. These include dividend models which focus on the present value of expected dividends, earnings models which focuses on the present value of expected earnings, and asset models which focus on the value of the company's assets.

Additionally, there are several other tests that analysts apply to balance sheets to determine the economic viability of a company.

The most common are:

§   Acid Test
§   Working Capital

The **Acid Test** ratio is computed by dividing the cash plus accounts receivables and short term investments by the current liabilities. It is a stringent test that indicates if a firm has enough short-term assets (without selling inventory) to cover its immediate liabilities. It is a similar, but more strenuous version of the working capital ratio, (indicating whether liabilities can be paid without selling inventory).

Companies with ratios of less than 1.00 cannot pay their current liabilities and should be looked at with extreme care. Furthermore, if the acid test ratio is much lower than the working capital ratio, it means current assets are highly dependent on inventory. Retail stores are examples of this type of business.

Working Capital ratio is determined by dividing a company's current assets by their liabilities. It indicates whether a firm has enough short-term assets to cover its immediate liabilities.

Things to remember:

If the ratio is less than **one** the company has negative working capital.

A high working capital ratio isn't always a good thing, it could indicate that they have too much inventory or they are not investing their excess cash.

In conclusion, there is no doubt that fundamental factors play a major role in a stock's price. However, if you form your price expectations based on fundamental factors, it is important that you study the price history as well or you may end up owning an undervalued stock that never recovers.

Simple Trading Strategies

Short Term

In today's volatile market it is possible to take a very short-term position and capture many price moves in each direction. Short term may be a little as a few minutes, hours or days. During that time frame, the stock may move considerably in both directions, allowing the flexible, active trader to profit.

For instance, using Microsoft, if you were bullish on Microsoft for the short term, you could buy the single stock futures contract and hold it until it reached your near-term objective. Let's say you bought the contract at 60 and in the following few days it moved to 64.50. You could then sell it and net 4.50 points in a very short period of time. That net 4.50 points would translate into a 33 1/3 percent gain based on the performance bond (margin) deposited with your broker.

If you thought that Microsoft was going down in the short-term, you could sell the single stock futures and try to buy it back when it fell to your objective. If you sold it at 60 and it rose to 65.00, then you would incur a loss of 5 points if you closed out your position (repurchased your contact). You could effect this short trade instantly because you wouldn't have to wait for an uptick as you would had you tried to short the actual Microsoft security. (This example is based on a 20% performance bond which at the time of this publication has not received regulatory approval.)

Of course, you would have to be right in predicting the price direction of Microsoft.

That's the simplest and easiest form of trading single stock futures.

Spreading Between Contracts

If a trader were bullish on Microsoft and bearish on IBM, they could buy the Microsoft futures contract and sell the IBM contract short. If and when the spread widens favorably, he could lift (liquidate) the respective contracts.

When narrow-based indices begin to trade, one could also be long the indices and short one or more single stock futures components depending their particular analysis. The possibilities are endless.

Traders could also put on spreads between different types of contracts, not necessarily in the same markets.

The are any number of combinations that one could use to hedge currency exposure as well. A Japanese trader long U.S. securities but worried about the exchange rate between the U.S. Dollar and the Japanese Yen could either be long or short the futures on the Yen and hedge whatever U.S. equities exposure he has by using single stock futures to hedge his exposure. This all depends upon which way the trader is leaning in his feeling toward the relationship

Longer Term

Single stock futures can be used by a trader with a slightly longer perspective. All futures contracts have an expiration month attached to them. Usually, financial futures have 4 expiration months, March, June, September and December with the final trading day sometime during the third week of the expiration month. Usually, the first month is the most liquid, with liquidity dropping off with each subsequent month.

Assuming depth of liquidity, a trader could take a position as far out as nine months. He could either trade it back and forth or just hold it until expiration. This strategy assumes enough liquidity at the more distant months.

Here's another strategy that is somewhat long term. The trader could be long (buy) the first month and near the expiration of that contract, sell it out and buy the next expiration month. This way the trader can hold the position continuously and still be in a liquid month. This is called rolling the position forward.

Single stock futures are contracts that may be settled in the physical delivery of the stock, where you would wind up being either long the stock and have to pay for it or having to deliver it if you were short.

Now, let's say you owned Microsoft, and didn't want to sell it but were getting nervous. To freeze your position and your risk, you could sell the single stock futures against all or a portion of your Microsoft position. This would suspend your risk. Here's how. Whichever way the stock moved, you would be making money on one position or another. For instance, if Microsoft went down, you would lose on the security position and gain on the short single stock futures position. And if Microsoft continued to go up, your stock position would gain by the same amount you would be losing on your short single stock futures position. The benefit of this strategy is that you would not have sold your stock, you would have frozen your risk, and would be able to take the position off when you felt more comfortable about the direction of Microsoft.

Arbitrageurs will move in and out of stock and single stock futures positions as these two instruments diverge from their rational values. This constant arbitrage keeps the value of the futures contract close to its "fair market value." Anytime the relationship between the security and the single stock future diverges beyond its theoretical value, a profitable trading opportunity would appear. Here's an example. If Microsoft suddenly was trading at 68 and the futures were trading at 66.50 at the same time, traders could buy the single stock futures and sell the stock locking in a known profit. The reason being is that at expiration, the prices of the two instruments would have to converge. They could also do the opposite is the futures were to suddenly move ahead of the stock price. They could buy the stock and sell the futures or deliver the actual stock.

Let's say the single stock futures were to rise suddenly and trade at 68 while Microsoft itself traded at 66.50, traders would rush in and sell the futures and buy the stock of Microsoft locking in a gross profit of 1.50 points. The important thing to keep in mind is that the futures and the actual price of the stock converge at expiration thus guaranteeing an automatic price-relationship self-righting mechanism by the actions of traders seeking to lock in the profits from this temporary divergence.

What Stocks Will Be Traded?

Initially, the exchanges offered single stock futures on the top, most actively traded securities but as time goes by and the contract proves to be overwhelmingly popular, more will be listed. When the Chicago Board Options Exchange (CBOE) started, options of less than 50 companies were initially listed. Now, over 25 years later, options on more than 1,500 separate securities are traded.

Here is a list of the stocks in each of the top indices. Only a handful have been selected for single stock futures trading but more will be listed as this product proves to be attractive to the investing and trading community.

STOCKS IN DOW JONES INDEX	STOCKS IN THE NASDAQ 100 INDEX
ALCOA INC	A D C TELECOM INC
AMERICAN EXPRESS	ABGENIX INC
AT&T CORP	ADELPHIA COMM CORP
BOEING CO	ADOBE SYSTEMS INC
CATERPILLAR INC	ALTERA CORP
CITIGROUP INC	AMAZON.COM INC
COCA-COLA CO	AMGEN INC
DISNEY (WALT)	ANDRX GROUP
DU PONT (EI)	APOLLO GROUP INC
EASTMAN KODAK	APPLE COMPUTER INC
EXXON MOBIL CORP	APPLIED COMPUTER INC
GENERAL ELECTRIC	APPLIED MATERIALS INC
GENERAL MOTORS CORP	APPLIED MICRO CIRUITS CP
HEWLETT-PACKARD	ARIBA INC
HOME DEPOT INC	ATMEL CORP
HONEYWELL INTERNATIONAL	BEA SYSTEMS INC
INTEL CORP	BED BATH & BEYOND INC
INTERNATIONAL BUSINESS MACHINES	BIOGEN INC
INTERNATIONAL PAPER CO	BIOMET INC
JOHNSON & JOHNSON	BROCADE COMMUNICATIONS SY
J P MORGAN CHASE	C I E N A CORP
MCDONALDS CORP	CHECK POINT SOFTWARE TECH
MERCK & CO	CHIRON CORP
MICROSOFT CORP	CINTAS CORP
MINNESOTA MINING	CISCO SYSTEMS INC
PHILIP MORRIS CO	CITRIX SYSTEMS INC
PROCTER & GAMBLE	CMGI INC
SBC COMMUNICATIONS	CNET NETWORKS INC
UNITED TECH CORP	COMCAST CORP
WAL-MART STORES	COMPUWARE CORP

COMVERSE TECHNOLOGY INC
CONCORD E F S INC
CONEXANT SYSTEMS INC
COSTCO WHOLESALE CORP
DELL COMPUTER CORP
EBAY INC
ECHOSTAR COMM CORP
ELECTRONIC ARTS INC
ERICSSON L M TEL CO
FISERV INC
FLEXTRONICS INTL LTD
GEMSTA
GENZYME CORP
GILEAD SCIENCES INC
HUMAN GENOME SCIENCES INC
I D E C PHARMACEUTICALS C
12 TECHNOLOGIES
IMMUNEX CORP
INKTOMI CORPORATION
INTEL CORP
INTUIT INC
JDS UNIPHASE CORP
JUNIPER NETWORKS
K L A TENCOR CORP
LEVEL 3 COMM INC
LINEAR TECHNOLOGY CORP
MAXIM INTEGRATED PROD INC
MCLEOD USA INCORP
MEDIMMUNE INC
MERCURY INTERACTIVE CORP
METROMEDIA FIBER NETWORK
MICROCHIP TECHNOLOGY INC
MICROSOFT CORP
MILLENNIUM PHARMACEUTICAL
MOLEX INC

NETWORK APPLIANCE CORP
NEXTEL COMM INC
NOVELL INC
NOVELLUS SYSTEMS INC
NVIDIA CORP
ORACLE CORP
P M C SIERRA INC
PACCAR INC
PALM INC
PANAMSAT CORP
PARAMETRIC TECH CORP
PAYCHEX INC
PEOPLESOFT INC
QLOGIC CORP
QUALCOMM INC
RATIONAL SOFTWARE CORP
REALNETWORKS INC
RF MICRO DEVICES INC
SANMINA-SCI CORP
SIEBEL SYSTEMS INC
SMURFIT STONE CONTAINER C
STAPLES INC
STARBUCKS CORP
SUN MICROSYSTEMS INC
T M P WORLDWIDE INC
TELLABS INC
THREE COM CORP/3COM CORP
U S A NETWORKS INC
VERISIGN INC
VERITAS SOFTWARE CORP DE
VITESSE SEMICONDUCTR CORP
WORLDCOM INC-WORLDCOM GRO
XILINK INC
YAHOO! INC

STOCKS IN THE S&P 500 INDEX

ABBOTT LABS
ADOBE SYSTEMS
ADVANCED MICRO DEVICES
AES CORP.
AETNA INC.
AFLAC CORPORATION
AIR PRODUCTS & CHEMICALS
AIRTOUCH COMMUNICATIONS
ALBERTO-CULVER
ALBERTSON'S
ALCAN ALUMINIUM LTD.
ALCOA INC.
ALLEGHENY TELEDYNE INC
ALLERGAN, INC.
ALLIEDSIGNAL
ALLSTATE CORP.

ALLTEL CORP.
ALZA CORP. CL. A
AMERADA HESS
AMEREN CORP.
AMERICA ONLINE
AMERICAN ELECTRIC POWER
AMERICAN EXPRESS
AMERICAN GENERAL
AMERICAN GREETINGS CL A
AMERICAN HOME PRODUCTS
AMERICAN INT'L. GROUP
AMERICAN STORES
AMERITECH
AMGEN
AMR CORP.
AMSOUTH BANCORPORATION

ANADARKO PETROLEUM
ANDREW CORP.
ANHEUSER-BUSCH
AON CORP.
APACHE CORP.
APPLE COMPUTER
APPLIED MATERIALS
ARCHER-DANIELS-MIDLAND
ARMSTRONG WORLD
ASARCO INC.
ASCEND COMMUNICATIONS
ASHLAND INC.
ASSOCIATES FIRST CAPITAL
AT&T CORP.
ATLANTIC RICHFIELD
AUTODESK, INC.
AUTOMATIC DATA PROCESSING INC.
AUTOZONE INC.
AVERY DENNISON CORP.
AVON PRODUCTS
BAKER HUGHES
BALL CORP.
BANK OF AMERICA CORP.
BANK OF NEW YORK
BANK ONE CORP.
BANKBOSTON CORP.
BANKERS TRUST CORP.
BARD (C.R.) INC.
BARRICK GOLD CORP.
BATTLE MOUNTAIN GOLD
BAUSCH & LOMB
BAXTER INTERNATIONAL INC.
BB&T CORPORATION
BEAR STEARNS COS.
BECTON, DICKINSON
BELL ATLANTIC
BELLSOUTH
BEMIS COMPANY
BESTFOODS INC.
BETHLEHEM STEEL
BIOMET, INC.
BLACK & DECKER CORP.
BLOCK H&R
BMC SOFTWARE
BOEING COMPANY
BOISE CASCADE
BOSTON SCIENTIFIC
BRIGGS & STRATTON
BRISTOL-MYERS SQUIBB
BROWN-FORMAN CORP.
BROWNING-FERRIS IND.
BRUNSWICK CORP.
BURLINGTON NORTHERN SANTA FE CORP.
BURLINGTON RESOURCES
CABLETRON SYSTEMS
CAMPBELL SOUP

CAPITAL ONE FINANCIAL
CARDINAL HEALTH, INC.
CARNIVAL CORP.
CAROLINA POWER & LIGHT
CASE CORP.
CATERPILLAR INC.
CBS CORP.
CENDANT CORPORATION
CENTEX CORP.
CENTRAL & SOUTH WEST
CENTURYTEL, INC.
CERIDIAN CORP.
CHAMPION INTERNATIONAL
CHARLES SCHWAB
CHASE MANHATTAN
CHEVRON CORP.
CHUBB CORP.
CIGNA CORP.
CINCINNATI FINANCIAL
CINERGY CORP.
CIRCUIT CITY GROUP
CISCO SYSTEMS
CITIGROUP INC.
CLEAR CHANNEL COMMUNICATIONS
CLOROX CO.
CMS ENERGY
COASTAL CORP.
COCA COLA CO.
COCA-COLA ENTERPRISES
COLGATE-PALMOLIVE
COLUMBIA ENERGY GROUP
COLUMBIA/HCA HEALTHCARE CORP.
K COMCAST CLASS A SPECIAL
COMERICA INC.
COMPAQ COMPUTER
COMPUTER ASSOCIATES INTL.
COMPUTER SCIENCES CORP.
COMPUWARE CORP.
CONAGRA INC.
CONSECO INC.
CONSOLIDATED EDISON HLDGS.
CONSOLIDATED NATURAL GAS
CONSOLIDATED STORES
CONSTELLATION ENERGY GROUP
COOPER INDUSTRIES
COOPER TIRE & RUBBER
COORS (ADOLPH)
CORNING INC.
COSTCO CO.
COUNTRYWIDE CREDIT INDUSTRIES
CRANE COMPANY
CROWN CORK & SEAL
CSX CORP.
CUMMINS ENGINE CO., INC.
CVS CORP.
CYPRUS AMAX MINERALS CO.

DANA CORP.
DANAHER CORP.
DARDEN RESTAURANTS
DATA GENERAL
DAYTON HUDSON
DEERE & CO.
DELL COMPUTER
DELPHI AUTOMOTIVE SYSTEMS
DELTA AIR LINES
DELUXE CORP.
DILLARD INC.
DOLLAR GENERAL
DOMINION RESOURCES
DONNELLEY (R.R.) & SONS
DOVER CORP.
DOW CHEMICAL
DOW JONES & CO.
DTE ENERGY CO.
DU PONT (E.I.)
DUKE ENERGY
DUN & BRADSTREET CORP. (NEW)
E G & G INC.
EASTERN ENTERPRISES
EASTMAN CHEMICAL
EASTMAN KODAK
EATON CORP.
ECOLAB INC.
EDISON INT'L
ELECTRONIC DATA SYSTEMS
EMC CORP.
EMERSON ELECTRIC
ENGELHARD CORP.
ENRON CORP.
ENTERGY CORP.
EQUIFAX INC.
EXXON CORP.
FANNIE MAE
FDX HOLDING CORP.
FEDERAL HOME LOAN MTG.
FEDERATED DEPT. STORES
FIFTH THIRD BANCORP
FIRST DATA
FIRST UNION CORP.
FIRSTAR CORPORATION
FIRSTENERGY CORP.
FLEET FINANCIAL GROUP
FLEETWOOD ENTERPRISES
FLUOR CORP.
FMC CORP.
FORD MOTOR
FORT JAMES CORP.
FORTUNE BRANDS, INC.
FOSTER WHEELER
FPL GROUP
FRANKLIN RESOURCES INC.
FREEPORT-MCMORAN COPPER & GOLD

FRONTIER CORP.
FRUIT OF THE LOOM LTD. HLDG. CO.
GANNETT CO.
GAP (THE)
GATEWAY, INC.
GENERAL DYNAMICS
GENERAL ELECTRIC
GENERAL INSTRUMENT CORP.
GENERAL MILLS
GENERAL MOTORS
GENUINE PARTS
GEORGIA-PACIFIC GROUP
GILLETTE CO.
GOLDEN WEST FINANCIAL
GOODRICH (B.F.)
GOODYEAR TIRE & RUBBER
GPU INC.
GRACE (W.R.) & CO.(NEW)
GRAINGER (W.W.) INC.
GREAT A & P
GREAT LAKES CHEMICAL
GTE CORP.
GUIDANT CORP.
HILLIBURTON CO.
HARCOURT GENERAL INC.
HARNISCHFEGER INDUS.
HARRAH'S ENTERTAINMENT
HARRIS CORP.
HARTFORD FINANCIAL SVC.GP.
HASBRO INC.
HCR MANOR CARE
HEALTHSOUTH CORP.
HEINZ (H.J.)
HELMERICH & PAYNE
HERCULES, INC.
HERSHEY FOODS
HEWLETT-PACKARD
HILTON HOTELS
HOME DEPOT
HOMESTAKE MINING
HONEYWELL
HOUSEHOLD INTERNATIONAL
HUMANA INC.
HUNTINGTON BANCSHARES
IKON OFFICE SOLUTIONS
ILLINOIS TOOL WORKS
IMS HEALTH INC.
INCO, LTD.
INGERSOLL-RAND
INTEL CORP.
INTERNATIONAL BUS. MACHINES
INTERNATIONAL FLAV/FRAG
INTERNATIONAL PAPER
INTERPUBLIC GROUP
ITT INDUSTRIES, INC.
JEFFERSON-PILOT

JOHNSON & JOHNSON
JOHNSON CONTROLS
JOSTENS INC.
K MART
KANSAS CITY SOUTHERN IND.
KAUFMAN & BROAD HOME CORP.
KELLOGG CO.
KERR-MCGEE
KEYCORP
KIMBERLY-CLARK
KING WORLD PRODUCTIONS
KLA-TENCOR CORP.
KNIGHT-RIDDER INC.
KOHL'S CORP.
KROGER CO.
LAIDLAW INC.
LEHMAN BROS. HLDGS.
LILLY (ELI) & CO.
LIMITED, THE
LINCOLN NATINAL
LIZ CLAIBORNE, INC.
LOCKHEED MARTIN CORP.
LOEWS CORP.
LONGS DRUG STORES
LOUISIANA PACIFIC
LOWE'S COS.
LSI LOGIC
LUCENT TECHNOLOGIES
MALLINCKRODT INC.
MARRIOTT INT'L.
MARSH & MCLENNAN
MASCO CORP.
MATTEL, INC.
MAY DEPT. STORES
MAYTAG CORP.
MBIA INC.
MBNA CORP.
MCDERMOTT INTERNATIONAL
MCDONALD'S CORP.
MCGRAW-HILL
MCI WORLDCOM
MCKESSON HBOC INC.
MEAD CORP.
MEDIAONE GROUP INC.
MEDTRONIC INC.
MELLON BANK CORP.
MERCANTILE BANCORP
MERCK & CO.
MEREDITH CORP.
MERRILL LYNCH
MGIC INVESTMENT
MICRON TECHNOLOGY
MICROSOFT CORP.
MILACRON INC.
MILLIPORE CORP.
MINNMINING & MFG.

MIRAGE RESORTS
MOBIL CORP.
MONSANTO COMPANY
MORGAN (J.P.) & CO.
MORGAN STANLEY, DEAN WITTER & CO.
MORTON INTERNATIONAL
MOTOROLA INC.
NACCO IND. CL. A
NALCO CHEMICAL
NATIONAL CITY CORP.
NATIONAL SEMICONDUCTOR
NATIONAL SERVICE IND.
NAVISTAR INTERNATIONAL CORP.
NEW CENTURY ENERGIES
NEW YORK TIMES CL. A
NEWELL RUBBERMAID INC.
NEWMONT MINING
NEXTEL COMMUNICATIONS
NIAGARA MOHAWK HLDGS INC.
NICOR INC.
NIKE INC.
NORDSTROM
NORFOLK SOUTHERN CORP.
NORTEL NETWORKS CORP.
NORTHERN STATES POWER
NORTHERN TRUST CORP.
NORTHROP GRUMMAN CORP.
NOVELL INC.
NUCOR CORP.
OCCIDENTAL PETROLEUM
OMNICOM GROUP
ONEOK INC.
ORACLE CORP.
OWENS CORNING
OWENS-ILLINOIS
PACCAR INC.
PACIFICORP
PALL CORP.
PARAMETRIC TECHNOLOGY
PARKER-HANNIFIN
PAYCHEX INC.
PE CORP. PE BIOSYSTEMS GROUP
PECO ENERGY CO.
PENNEY (J.C.)
PEOPLES ENERGY
PEOPLESOFT INC.
PEP BOYS
PEPSICO INC.
PFIZER, INC.
PG&E CORP.
PHARMACIA & UPJOHN, INC.
PHELPS DODGE
PHILIP MORRIS
PHILLIPS PETROLEUM
PIONEER HI-BRED INT'L
PITNEY-BOWES

PLACER DOME INC.
PNC BANK CORP.
POLAROID CORP.
POTLATCH CORP.
PP & L RESOURCES
PPG INDUSTRIES
PRAXAIR, INC.
PROCTER & GAMBLE
PROGRESSIVE CORP.
PROVIDENT COMPANIES INC.
PROVIDIAN FINANCIAL CORP.
PUBLIC SERV. ENTERPRISE INC.
PULTE CORP.
QUAKER OATS
RALSTON-RALSTON PURINA GP
RAYCHEM CORP.
B RAYTHEON CO.
REEBOK INTERNATIONAL
REGIONS FINANCIAL CORP.
RELIANT ENERGY
REPUBLIC NEW YORK
REYNOLDS METALS
RITE AID
RJR NABISCO HOLDINGS CORP.
ROCKWELL INTERNATIONAL
ROHM & HAAS
ROWAN COS.
ROYAL DUTCH PETROLEUM
RUSSELL CORP.
RYDER SYSTEM
SAFECO CORP.
SAFEWAY INC.
SARA LEE CORP.
SBC COMMUNICATIONS INC.
SCHERING-PLOUGH
SCHLUMBERGER LTD.
SCIENTIFIC-ATLANTA
SEAGATE TECHNOLOGY
SEAGRAM CO. LTD.
SEALED AIR CORP.
SEARS, ROEBUCK & CO.
SEMPRA ENERGY
SERVICE CORP. INTERNATIONAL
SHARED MEDICAL SYSTEMS
SHERWIN-WILLIAMS
SIGMA-ALDRICH
SILICON GRAPHICS
SLM HOLDING CORP.
SNAP-ON INC.
SOLECTRON
SONAT INC.
SOUTHERN CO.
SOUTHTRUST CORP.
SOUTHWEST AIRLINES
SPRINGS INDUSTRIES INC.

SPRINT CORP. FON GROUP
SPRINT CORP. PCS GROUP
ST. JUDE MEDICAL
ST. PAUL COS.
STANLEY WORKS
STAPLES INC.
STATE STREET CORP.
SUMMIT BANCORP
SUN MICROSYSTEMS
SUNOCO INC.
SUNTRUST BANKS
SUPERVALU INC.
SYNOVUS FINANCIAL
SYSCO CORP.
TANDY CORP.
TEKTRONIX INCL.
TELLABS, INC.
TEMPLE-INLAND
TENET HEALTHCARE CORP.
TENNECO INC.
TEXACO INC.
TEXAS INSTRUMENTS
TEXAS UTILITIES HLDG.COS.
TEXTRON INC.
THERMO ELECTRON
THOMAS & BETTS
TIME WARNER INC.
TIMES MIRROR
TIMKEN CO.
TJX COMPANIES INC.
TORCHMARK CORP.
TOYS R US HLDG. COS.
TRANSAMERICA CORP.
TRIBUNE CO.
TRICON GLOBAL RESTAURANTS
TRW INC.
TUPPERWARE CORP.
TYCO INTERNATIONAL
U.S. BANCORP
UNICOM CORP.
UNILEVER N.V.
UNION CARBIDE
UNION PACIFIC
UNION PACIFIC RESOURCES GROUP
UNION PLANTERS
UNISYS CORP.
UNITED HEALTHCARE CORP.
UNITED TECHNOLOGIES
UNOCAL CORP.
UNUM CORP.
US WEST INC.
USAIRWAYS GROUP INC.
UST INC.
USX-MARATHON GROUP
USX-U.S. STEEL GROUP
V.F. CORP.

B VIACOM INC.	WENDY'S INTERNATIONAL
WACHOVIA CORP.	WESTVACO CORP.
WAL-MART STORES	WEYERHAEUSER CORP.
WALGREEN CO.	WHIRLPOOL CORP.
WALT DISNEY CO.	WILLAMETTE INDUSTRIES
WARNER-LAMBERT	WILLIAMS COS.
WASHINGTON MUTUAL, INC.	WINN-DIXIE
WASTE MANAGEMENT	WORTHINGTON IND.
WATSON PHARMACEUTICALS	WRIGLEY (WM) JR.
WELLS FARGO & CO.	XEROX CORP.

The universe for potential single stock futures products is enormous and with time will include many of these companies. However, the initial array includes the most actively traded stocks.

Brokerage Houses

Single stock futures contracts are available through both Broker Dealers (traditional securities firms) and firms dealing exclusively with futures products. These firms are known as Futures Commissions Merchants (FCM) and are regulated by the Commodities Futures Trading Commission.

Each brokerage firm has stringent rules as to how much money must be placed in your account. Suitability rules, margin rules, & maintenance rules can vary between firms but can be set no less than the exchange minimum rules.

Deciding which type of account to trade these instruments has to be considered by the customer as there is a difference in the type of protection covered under the customer account agreement

The Securities and Exchange Commission has jurisdictional authority over broker dealers. All accounts at broker-dealers are SIPC guaranteed. SIPC is the nonprofit corporation created by an act of Congress to protect clients of brokerage firms that are forced into bankruptcy. Membership is composed of all brokers and dealers registered under the Securities Exchange Act of 1934, all members of securities exchanges and most NASD members.

SIPC provides brokerage customers up to $500,000 coverage for cash and securities held by the firms (although coverage of cash is limited to $100,000).

It is best to check with your broker to get the details on the differences between the two types of accounts where single stock futures can be traded.

Futures Commission Merchants (FCM's) are brokerage firms that deal in products offered on futures exchanges. They should be very familiar with all of the aspects of futures trading.

Like stock brokerage firms, they too have rules for opening accounts, including minimum capital requirements and suitability rules. Customer funds are kept in segregated accounts. The various clearing firms are regulated by the exchanges and subject to the capital rules of their designated self-regulatory organization (DRSO). There are very tight financial safeguards that all firms must meet.

Like security firms, they can raise the minimum capital requirement for trading single stock futures. The exchanges set the minimum performance bond (margin) requirements but the individual firms can raise them to meet their own financial safeguards.

Your account is treated as a futures trading account where all customer funds are kept segregated from the firm's capital.

Electronic Trading
Where does your single stock futures order go?

If your order is entered electronically, it is routed to the order-matching engine of the exchange where the desired single stock futures is listed. It usually only takes a few seconds to get price reports for market orders. It is a very quick turn around time which makes electronic order entry a popular tool. Many brokerage firms have an electronic interface with the various order matching engines of the competing exchanges.

If your order is phoned in, it will be entered by your broker into their electronic order entry system and routed to the proper exchange for execution. Your broker will get a confirmation of the fill and will call you with a report. Your order may be have to be checked to see if you have enough margin money (performance bond) in your account to cover the transaction. Then, it is placed into the order routing system for execution. This extra little step adds to the time for your order to reach the marketplace. If speed is an important consideration, you should look into setting up an account so that your orders can be entered by you through the order entry interface provided by your brokerage firm.

Some orders will be executed in trading pits and the order is then phoned or electronically transmitted to the exchange where the desired single stock futures is traded. It is then given to a floor broker who executes the trade according to your instructions.

After the order is filled, the order is returned to the firm for their record keeping and the execution price is relayed to you. It is obvious that there are many more steps to getting the order filled than an order that is entered electronically directly into an exchanges order matching engine.

Additional news events that you should be aware of that can cause sudden jumps in the price of the underlying security of the single stock futures that you are trading.

Many corporate news events can affect the price of the underlying security of a single stock futures contract. Earnings are released every quarter, usually at the end of the trading day in the first week of the new quarter. Disappointing earnings can cause a big downward move in the price of the underlying security that will quickly be reflected in the single stock futures causing large gaps to occur. A stock may close at 60 but disappointing earnings may cause it to reopen the next day 10 points or more lower.

It does happen and the effect can be very damaging to your position. It is also possible that the earnings are very positive and also result in a strong upward movement. So, a word to the wise. Be aware when your stock's earning announcements are due.

Companies often issue profit warnings that can cause a sudden drop in the price of their stock. The warnings are usually given to cushion investors expectations and are based on that companies projected expectations of their sales and other factors that each industry factors into their earnings projections. In declining markets, downward earnings projections are common.

Security analysts follow individual companies and often issue reports about their prospects as well as earnings projections. If an analyst suddenly upgrades or downgrades his earnings estimate of an individual company, major moves often follow. These reports are often released during the trading day.

The trader should always be aware of government reports like unemployment numbers, producer and consumer price indices, Beige Book reports of the Federal Reserve Bank, purchasing agents indication and others reports as they can cause a gigantic movement if there are major surprises attached to these numbers.

The **producer price index** is an inflationary indicator published by the U.S. Bureau of Labor Statistics to evaluate wholesale price levels in the economy and often foreshadows economic activity in futures months. The **consumer price index** is an inflationary indicator that measures the change in the cost of a fixed basket of products and services, including housing, electricity, food, and transportation. The CPI (also called the cost-of-living index) is published monthly. A very important report is released monthly by the Department of Labor that measures **unemployment figures.** This report can move the market quickly when announced.

You should get a economic calendar so that you can be aware of the dates when reports will be issued. Barrons carries the calendar for the coming week's reports, as do many brokerage firms web sites.

Odds and Ends

Single stock futures contracts can be purchased and sold in seconds or held as long as the trader desires but no longer than the contract's maturity. Most futures contracts are not held to maturity but are closed out well in advance of the settlement date.

The prices of single stock futures will be available in the Wall Street Journal and other leading business publications. Look in the commodity section of the financial pages of your newspaper. Quote vendors like Bloomberg, FutureSource, e-Signal, PC Quote *et al* will make them available on a real-time basis to their subscribers.

Single stock futures prices for contracts on foreign exchanges are usually available in the business section of each country's daily newspapers in larger metropolitan cities. For instance, single stock futures traded in Singapore can be checked in such newspapers as Straits Times and Business Times. LIFFE contract prices will be available in the London Financial Times.

Naturally, if a merger or acquisition takes place that affects the underlying security, the exchanges will adjust the contract to reflect these changes.

It should be remembered that if the underlying security stops trading, the single stock futures will also stop trading and resume when that stock begins trading again. It is the same as if you were trading securities or options. When the underlying security or securities have a trading halt, all derivatives products stop trading almost immediately.

You do not have to own the underlying security to trade the single stock futures contract. Just remember though that at settlement date, if you are still long the contract, you will become long the underlying security. And conversely, if you are short the contract, you will have to make delivery of the shares if it is settled physically.

Chapter 4

WHERE TO TRADE SINGLE STOCK FUTURES

History of Single Stock Futures Trading Prior To the Passage of the Commodities Modernization Act of 2000.

Single stock futures have been trading since the early 1990's on exchanges outside the United States. They have met with varying degrees of success. With the exception of the London International Financial Futures Exchange (LIFFE), these exchanges have initially concentrated on the stocks of companies located within their own borders.

Single stock futures are now traded on exchanges throughout the world, the following is a sample of where they are traded.

1. **Australia**
2. **Hong Kong**
3. **Spain**
4. **Finland**
5. **Mexico**
6. **U.K.**
7. **Canada**
8. **Singapore**

When LIFFE announced that they were going to trade single stock futures on 7 American companies and recently expanded to the following 20:

1. American International Group Inc.
2. Amgen Inc.
3. AOL Time Warner Inc.
4. Bristo-Myers Squibb Co.
5. Cisco Systems Inc.
6.   Citigroup Inc.
7. EMC Corporation
8. Exxon Mobil Corp.
9. General Electric Company
10. IBM Corporation
11. Intel Corp.
12. JDS Uniphase Corp.
13. Juniper Networks Inc.
14. Merck & Co. Inc.
15. Microsoft Corp.
16. Oracle Corporation
17. Pfizer Inc.
18. Qualcomm Inc.
19. Sun Microsystems Inc.
20. Wal-Mart Stores Inc.

They set the ball in motion for Congress to act swiftly to allow trading of single stock futures in the United States lest this market develop in Europe. LIFFE might have first mover advantage but the marketing abilities of U.S. futures, options, and securities exchanges will probably extinguish that advantage as the product becomes actively traded in the United States.

Exchange Alliances Formed

With the passage of the CFMA of 2000, the exchanges began to scramble for alliances that would give them expertise and market liquidity, as well as marketing muscle.

Chicago Exchanges Join Forces

The **earliest** of the alliances to trade single stock futures is the joint venture between the **Chicago Mercantile Exchange (CME), the Chicago Board Options Exchange (CBOE), and the Chicago Board of Trade (CBOT).** The three big Chicago exchanges created a new, all-electronic exchange devoted exclusively to trading single stock futures The joint venture will be a for-profit company with its own management and board and will be separately organized as a regulated exchange.

Single stock futures will be traded electronically on the joint venture exchange, and orders may be entered through both the new CBOEdirect™ electronic platform and CME's GLOBEX®2 electronic trading system. CBOT traders will have full access to trade the products, adding to the market's liquidity.

Each of these exchanges brings a vast amount of experience in trading equity index products which should make their newly created exchange a very formidable player in the new world of single stock futures

The Chicago Board Options Exchange created and launched the first listed options on stocks in 1973 and the first index options in 1982. Today, CBOE lists options on more than 1,500 stocks and on over 40 indices, such as the S&P 500, the Dow Jones Industrial Average , the Russell 2000, the Nasdaq-100, and the S&P 100. It remains the world's largest and most successful options marketplace.

Chicago Mercantile Exchange Inc. launched the first successful stock index futures contracts on the S&P 500 in 1982. Today, CME trades futures and futures options on indexes including the S&P 500, Nasdaq-100, S&P MidCap 400, Russell 2000, FORTUNE e-500, S&P/BARRA Growth and Value Indexes, and Nikkei 225, as well as its electronically traded E-mini S&P 500 and E-mini Nasdaq-100 contracts (these were the fastest growing products in the exchange's history). CME also trades interest rate, foreign exchange and commodity products

The CBOT has an established and active market in equities through its Dow Jones Industrial Average futures and options products, which trade via open outcry and on the exchange's electronic trading platform. The CBOT's equities sector has expanded with the launch of its mini-sized DJIA futures on September 30, 2001, and its Dow Jones-AIG Commodity Index in the fourth quarter of 2001, both on the exchange's electronic platform. In addition, the CBOT provides a diverse mix of more than 60 futures and futures-options contract markets for major agricultural and a broad range of interest rate products via its open outcry and electronic trading platforms.

NASDAQ/LIFFE Form A Partnership To Trade Single Stock Futures

London International Financial Futures and Options Exchange (LIFFE), a leading electronic derivatives exchange, and The NASDAQ, the world's leading electronic stock market, formed an exchange to develop the single stock futures market also based on global stocks, for U.S. and European customers. These products will be listed on LIFFE CONNECT™, LIFFE's electronic trading platform.

LIFFE and Nasdaq will form a U.S.-regulated entity, which will list single stock futures on global companies through LIFFE CONNECT™, for trading by U.S. customers.

NASDAQ/LIFFE Markets (NQLX) offer single stock futures that differ from the LIFFE universal stock futures that are available on LIFFE. The single stock futures offered by NASDAQ/LIFFE Markets will try to build on the successes of the LIFFE stock futures product, universal stock futures.

However, differences do exist between the two products, largely reflecting the underlying markets in which they operate. For example, NASDAQ/LIFFE Markets single stock futures were initially be based primarily on U.S. companies, whereas the LIFFE universal stock futures product offering has a much heavier European focus with contracts spread across UK, Continental Europe and some U.S. companies.

Additionally, the NQLX single stock futures are physically settled whereas the LIFFE universal stock futures are cash settled.

Only traders registered to NASDAQ/LIFFE Markets member firms may trade directly on the Exchange. Private investor business is generally transacted on the market through brokers who are registered as member firms.

The **American Stock Exchange** has also indicated that it too will gear up for trading in single stock futures but through a combination of electronic order entry and open-outcry on the floor of the exchange.

Another competitor for single stock futures business is Island Futures Exchange LLC, part of the Island ECN Inc. or electronic communications network, which filed late in 2001 with the Commodity Futures Trading Commission to list security futures products.

Island is best known as an electronic market place for matching stock and exchange-traded fund bids and offers, filed to become a CFTC-regulated fully registered contract market.

Island, which has more than 700 broker dealers, made the move because of the extreme interest in this product by its membership.

Without a doubt, more electronic communications networks (ECN'S) will move to become fully registered contract marketplaces as the product lives up to it's expectations.

If and when other exchanges begin to stake out their share of the single stock futures markets, trading volume in this new product will rapidly expand. Should the competing, identical contracts on the various exchanges become interchangeable (fungible), additional liquidity will be created.

Chapter 5

Contract Specifications

All futures contracts have specifications that delineate the terms of the contract. Generally these terms include the following features:

Contract Size

The specified quantity of the underlying traded market; so many pounds, shares, etc.

Contract Months

The specific month in which delivery may take place under the terms of a futures contract. Also referred to as delivery month. Specifies the month in which the contracts settle.

Contract Expiration

The final day when trading may occur in a given futures or option contract month.

Minimum Price Movement

The smallest allowable increment of price movement for a contract. A contract may move in more than one tick at a time.

Maximum Price Movement

The largest price movement allowed in a day.

Tick Value

The dollar value of each tick.

Settlement Method

Futures contracts outstanding at the end of the last trading day must be settled by either physical delivery or cash settled, depending on the exchanges contract.

Trading Hours

The time period within which the instrument is allowed to trade.

OneChicago
United States

Contract Specifications
Single Stock Futures

Contract Size:	100 shares of the underlying security
Minimum Price Move:	$0.01 or $1.00 per contract
Maximum Price Move:	Coordinated with the underlying market
Contract Months:	Five quarterly and two serial months (the first three calendar months are always listed)
Contract Expiration:	The third Friday of delivery month
Settlement Method:	Physical Delivery
Trading Hours:	Initially 8:30 am - 3:02 pm

HAS NOT RECEIVED REGULATORY APPROVAL

NASDAQ/LIFFE (NQLX)
United States

Contract Specifications
Single Stock Futures

Contract Size:	100 shares of the underlying security
Minimum Price Move:	$0.01 or $1.00 per contract
Maximum Price Move:	Coordinated with the underlying market
Contract Months:	Five quarterly and two serial months (the first three calendar months are always listed)
Contract Expiration:	The third Friday of delivery month
Settlement Method:	Physical Delivery
Trading Hours:	Initially 8:30 am - 3:02 pm

HAS NOT RECEIVED REGULATORY APPROVAL

American Stock Exchange
United States

Contract Specifications
Single Stock Futures

Contract Size:	100 shares of the underlying security
Minimum Price Move:	Undecided
Maximum Price Move:	Coordinated with the underlying market
Contract Months:	Aligned with Amex stock options
Contract Expiration:	Aligned with Amex stock options
Settlement Method:	Physical settlement
Trading Hours:	Initially 9:30 am - 4:02 pm EST

HAS NOT RECEIVED REGULATORY APPROVAL

Island Futures Exchange
United States

Contract Specifications
Single Stock Futures

Contract Size:	100 shares of the underlying company
Minimum Price Move:	Possibly 1/10 cent or $0.01
Maximum Price Move:	Coordinated with the underlying market
Contract Months:	Undecided
Contract Expiration:	Undecided
Settlement Method:	Physical delivery
Trading Hours:	7:00 am - 8:00 pm

HAS NOT RECEIVED REGULATORY APPROVAL

LIFFE
U.K.

Contract Specifications
Single Stock Futures
U.S. Shares

Contract Size:	100 shares of the underlying security
Minimum Price Move:	$0.01 or $1.00 per contract
Maximum Price Move:	Coordinated with the underlying market
Contract Months:	Nearest two months of March, June, September, December, plus nearest two serial months
Contract Expiration:	The third Friday of the expiration month
Settlement Method:	Physical Delivery
Trading Hours:	08:00 - 18:00 (London Time)

LIFFE
U.K.

Contract Specifications
Single Stock Futures
Continental European Shares

Contract Size:	100 shares of underlying company 1000 shares of underlying company- Italian futures
Minimum Price Move:	1 eurocent Sweden SK 0.01, Switzerland CHF 0.1
Maximum Price Move:	Coordinated with the underlying market
Contract Months:	Nearest two months of March, June, September, December, plus nearest two serial months
Contract Expiration:	Third Friday of the delivery month, France: Penultimate business day of delivery month, Italy: business day preceding third Friday of delivery month
Settlement Method:	Cash Settled
Trading Hours:	Finland: 08:00-16:30 France Italy, Netherlands, Spain, Sweden, Switzerland: 08:00-16:00. Germany: 08:00-18:00

LIFFE
U.K.

Contract Specifications
Single Stock Futures
U.K. Shares

Contract Size:	1000 shares of underlying company
Minimum Price Move:	0.5 pence
Maximum Price Move:	Coordinated with the underlying market
Contract Months:	Nearest two months of March, June, September, December, plus nearest two serial months
Contract Expiration:	Third Wednesday of the delivery month
Settlement Method:	Cash Settled
Trading Hours:	08:00-16:30 (London time)

HEX Plc
Finland

Contract Specifications
Single Stock Futures

Contract Size:	100 shares of the underlying company
Minimum Price Move:	1 eurocent
Maximum Price:	None
Contract Months:	All, upon demand
Contract Expiration:	The third Friday of the expiration month
Settlement Method:	Physical delivery
Trading Hours:	10:00 am - 9:00 pm

Hong Kong Exchange and Clearing Limited (HKEx)
China

Contract Specifications
Single Stock Futures

Contract Size:	Varies on underlying company 1,10,100,1000 shares
Minimum Price Move:	US company US$0.01 Japan 1JPY or 1000 JPY South Korea 1 KRW or 100 KRW, Taiwan NT$0.01
Maximum Price Move:	Cordinated with underlying market
Contract Months:	Spot, next two calendar months, next two calendar quarters
Contract Expiration:	U.S. The third Friday, all others Hong Kong business day preceding last business day of contract month
Settlement Method:	All cash settled in US Dollars
Trading Hours:	US company 8:00-17:00, South Korea 8:00-14:00 Japan 8:00-14:00 Taiwan 8:00-13:30

MEFF
Spain

Contract Specifications
Single Stock Futures

Contract Size:	100 shares in the underlying company
Minimum Price Move:	1 eurocent
Maximum Price Move:	None
Contract Month:	At least four expiration months in the March–June- September–December cycle
Contract Expiration:	The third Friday of the Expiration Date
Settlement Method:	Physical Delivery
Trading Hours:	From 9:00 to 17:35 hours

Mercado Mexicano de Derivados (MEXDER)
Mexico

Contract Specifications
Single Stock Futures

Contract Size:	1,000 Shares in the underlying company
Minimum Price Move:	.001 pesos
Maximum Price Move:	None
Contract Months:	March, June, September, December
Contract Expiration:	Fourth Thursday of the month it expires
Settlement Method:	Physical Delivery
Trading Hours:	7:30 am - 15:00 hours

Bourse de Montreal
Canada

Contract Specifications
Single Stock Futures

Contract Size:	100 shares of the underlying company
Minimum Price Move:	Canadian stocks: C$0.01 per contract International stocks: prices in the currency of the underlying stock
Maximum Price Move:	A trading halt in conjunction with the halt in the underlying stock
Contract Months:	Quarterly and serial contract months to coincide with equity option contract months
Contract Expiration:	Canadian stocks: 4:00 pm on the third Friday of the contract month.
Settlement Method:	Canadian stocks: Physical delivery International: Cash Settlement
Trading Hours:	8:30 am to 4:15 pm (EST/EDT)

Singapore Exchange (SGX)

Contract Specifications
Single Stock Futures

Contract Size:	1,000 shares of the underlying company
Minimum Price Move:	SGD 0.01 per share
Maximum Price Move:	None
Contract Months:	3 nearest months (Example Dec, Jan, Feb)
Contract Expiration:	The second last business day of the contract month.
Settlement Method:	Cash Settlement
Trading Hours:	9:00 am-12:30 pm Singapore time 2:00 pm to 5:00 pm Singapore time

Sydney Futures Exchange Limited (SFE)
Australia

Contract Specifications
Single Stock Futures

Contract Size:	1,000 shares in the underlying company
Minimum Price Move:	1 cent per share = A$10.00 per contract
Maximum Price Move:	None
Contract Months:	One either – Jan/Apr/Jul/Oct or Feb/May/Aug/Nov or Mar/Jun/Sep/Dec expiration cycles
Contract Expiration:	Trading ceases at 4:30 pm on the Thursday immediately preceding the last Friday of the settlement month
Settlement Method:	Physically deliverable or cash settled
Trading Hours:	5:10 pm – 7:30 am* 9:50 am – 4:30 pm *7:00 am during US Daylight Savings

Part 3

Behind the Scenes

Chapter 6

Modernizing the CEA

It was noted earlier that single stock futures were banned in the United States in 1982 when the two regulatory agencies (Commodities Futures Trading Commission and the Securities and Exchange Commission) could not resolve their jurisdictional authority questions of single stock futures and narrow-based indices. Rather than hold up the launch of broader-based security indices, the two agencies agreed to a "moratorium" on the question. It became known as the Shad/Johnson accord and was named after the respective chairmen, Phillip Johnson of the CFTC and John Shad of the SEC.

In 1982, SEC Chairman John Shad reached an agreement with CFTC Chairman Phil Johnson on the regulation of certain derivative instruments. This agreement, known as the Shad-Johnson Accord, soon thereafter approved by Congress, treated options on securities or on a securities index as themselves securities (under the SEC) but treated futures on a broad-based index as futures (under the CFTC). It prohibited single stock futures and narrow-based indices.

This agreement removed the road blocks for the introduction of futures contracts on broad based indices such as the Standard and Poor's 500 Stock Index contract at the Chicago Mercantile Exchange and the Value Line Index at the Kansas City Board of Trade.

While there were many critics of the accord from its inception, it remained in place until the passage of the Commodities Futures Modernization Act of 2000 which removed the restrictions on trading single stock futures and narrow-based indices on regulated exchanges.

The futures industry wanted to be able to trade these products and be on a competitive footing with foreign exchanges. They told their story to Congress and it was heard. One of the major concerns of the exchanges was the fear that the U.S. would lose the market for single stock futures to foreign exchanges, especially London's LIFFE which had plans to launch universal stock futures (their version of single stock futures) on several major American companies listed on the New York Stock Exchange.

Previously, most foreign exchanges just traded their version of single stock futures on companies located within their own borders.

House and Senate Hearings

In November 1999, the President's Working Group announced its view that single stock futures can be a valuable risk-management too, both for institutional and individual investors and suggested that the prohibition on such futures be lifted.

In November 1999, the President's Working Group on Financial Markets presented its report, *Over-the-Counter Derivatives Markets and the Commodity Exchange Act*, to Congress. In this report, the Working Group, chaired by Secretary Summers and the Chairmen of the Federal Reserve, the Commodity Futures Trading Commission and the Securities and Exchange Commission, set forth a series of unanimous recommendations designed to reform the legal and regulatory framework affecting the OTC derivatives market.

Specifically, H.R. 4541, included provisions for the treatment of OTC derivatives, regulatory relief for the futures exchanges, and the reform of the Shad-Johnson restrictions on the trading of single stock and narrow-based stock index futures.

Another provision of the Commodities Futures Modernization Act (CFMA) provided not only for the authorization of the trading of single stock futures but also *Narrow-Based Indices* that would be allowed to trade on both futures and securities exchanges, subject to coordinated regulation by the SEC and the CFTC. Futures based on broad baskets of securities would, as permitted under prior law, continue to trade solely on futures exchanges subject to CFTC jurisdiction.

Under the new definition, an index is narrow-based only if it contains fewer than nine component securities, if a component security comprises more than 30% of its weighting, or if the five highest-weighted component securities in the aggregate comprise more than 60% of its weighting.

Because the definition of a narrow-based index had changed, the overwhelming majority of exchange-listed index options now count as "broad-based." This was good news for most index investors because broad-based index derivatives receive a more generous tax treatment than narrow-based indices or exchange-traded funds based on those indices.

The CFTC and SEC then agreed to develop a detailed legislative proposal to deal with this phenomenon. Pressure was put on these two agencies to come up with a workable agreement or have the Senate impose its own rules. The fact that the CFTC would be out of business on September 30, 2000 if Congress didn't reauthorize the agency helped mend the fences between these two regulatory bodies.

With the help of the mediation efforts of Secretary of the Treasury Lawrence Summers, the two agencies finally resolved their jurisdictional dispute. In early September 2000, the Commodity Futures Trading Commission and the Securities & Exchange Commission announced that they had reached an agreement on the regulation of single stock futures and narrow-based stock indices. Their long-running jurisdictional dispute on these points had been a substantial obstacle to Congressional reauthorization of the Commodity Exchange Act.

With the working relationship between the SEC and the CFTC regarding the jurisdiction of single stock futures and narrow based-indices resolved, Congress passed the Commodities Futures Modernization Act of 2000 that set the start date for trading in these instruments so that qualified institutions could begin trading them on August 18, 2001 and individuals could begin on December 26, 2001. Thus a major stumbling block to the launching of these exciting instruments was removed.

Chapter 7

THE TERMS OF THE SHAD-JOHNSON IMPASSE RESOLUTION

Developments that helped resolve the impasse that resulted in the Shad-Johnson Accord in 1982 are presented in this chapter as well as discussion of tax considerations.

The agreement provides for joint jurisdiction between the CFTC and the SEC over single stock futures and narrow-based stock indices, both defined as security futures. Broad-based indices, as defined below, will remain under the CFTC's jurisdiction.

Broad-Based Stock Indices

If a futures contract on a stock index satisfies either of the criteria set forth in Path A or Path B below, it qualifies as a broad-based index under the exclusive jurisdiction of the CFTC:

"Path A" defines a broad-based index as one that has:

1.   Ten or more securities

2.   No single component constituting more than 30% of the weighting

3.   The five largest components by weight collectively constituting no more than 60% of the weighting;

4.   The bottom quarter of component stocks with a combined average daily dollar trading volume of more than $50 million, or $30 million if the index includes at least 15 securities.

"Path B" alternatively defines a broad based index as one that has:

1.   Nine or more securities;
2.   No component constituting more than 30% of the weighting;
3.   Each component qualifying as a "large" stock (defined as one of the top 500 stocks common to rankings of both the largest market capitalization and largest average daily trading volume).

An index that does not qualify as "broad-based" under either Path A or Path B would be defined as a security future subject to the joint jurisdiction of the CFTC and SEC.

Joint Jurisdiction over Security Futures

The CFTC would be the primary regulator of futures markets and futures commission merchants ("FCMs"); the SEC would be the primary regulator of securities markets and broker-dealers.

To trade security futures, futures exchanges and FCMs would be required to file notice registration with the SEC, and securities exchanges and broker dealers would be required to file notice registration with the CFTC.

All exchanges and intermediaries that trade security futures would be regulated by both the SEC and CFTC, but only core provisions of each agency's statutes would apply to notice registrants.

Notice registration provides that for the limited purpose relating to the sale of single stock futures, FCM's can "passport" into registration with the SEC and broker-dealers can "passport" into registration with the CFTC. Those that are eligable can file a one page notice form 7R for registration with the CFTC and form BD-N for SEC.

Futures exchanges would be required to file with the SEC, subject to an expedited rule filing process, rule changes that relate to security futures. The rule filing with the SEC could be made after the effective date of the rule if adopted by the futures exchange under certification to the CFTC, but remains subject to abrogation by the SEC after consultation with the CFTC. Similarly, securities exchanges would be subject to the CFTC's rule review and disapproval provisions.

Designated contract markets would be subject to inspection by both agencies at any time as deemed appropriate. To avoid duplicative and inconsistent regulation, the SEC is required to coordinate with the CFTC on examinations of SEC notice-registered exchanges and broker-dealers, and the CFTC would coordinate with the SEC on examinations of CFTC notice-registered markets and intermediaries.

The National Futures Association ("NFA") would be permitted to register as a national securities association for the limited purpose of regulating activities of notice-registered broker-dealers. In such capacity, the NFA would develop suitability and other sales practice rules comparable to those applicable to securities transactions and would test its members for knowledge of securities laws.

Segregation requirements under CFTC rules would apply to customers' security futures positions held in futures accounts maintained by FCMs. Securities Investor Protection Corporation ("SIPC") insurance coverage would extend to customers' security futures positions held in securities accounts maintained by broker-dealers.

Mandatory Linked Clearing Facilities

Linked clearing of fungible securities on security futures by futures and securities clearinghouses will be mandatory through joint rulemaking on the later of:

Two years after trading commences in any security future; or the date on which the market is deemed to be viable (180 days after the first month in which average aggregate comparable share volume of single stock futures equals or exceeds 10% of average aggregate comparable share volume of options on equity securities).

"Section 31" Transaction Fees

Transaction fees which are normally charged on securities transactions pursuant to section 31 of the Securities Exchange Act would not apply to security futures.

Margins on Security Futures

Pending final approval, margin requirements for security futures would be the higher of: margin requirements for comparable option contracts, exclusive of premium, or the amount required by the applicable exchange using its risk-based portfolio margining system.

Large Trader Reporting

CFTC large trader reporting requirements would apply to securities exchanges and broker-dealers that trade security futures.

Tax Treatment

Security futures would be permitted to trade on the date the Secretary of the Treasury certifies that the tax treatment applicable to security futures is equivalent to equity options (but not earlier that one year after enactment of the Commodity Futures Modernization Act of 2000); or on January 2, 2003 if the disparity between tax treatment is not resolved. Security futures would be permitted to trade for two years under the current tax treatment, subject to a sunset provision if Congress has not resolved the tax treatment disparity.

Dual Trading Restriction

The CFTC will issue regulations to prohibit dual trading in security futures on contract markets, subject to limited exceptions

Actual Tax Treatment

Tax Treatment of Futures Contracts

The following discussion should not be construed as tax planning advice. Only your accountant or tax advisor should be relied upon for definitive answers regarding the tax consequences of your single stock future transactions.

There are significant tax differences between stock, futures and single stock futures transactions. Let's talk about tax treatment of stocks first.

Depending upon the holding period, your stock transactions are either taxed at short term or long term capital gains. The tax consequences come into effect when you actually close out your transactions. Normally, if you hold your stock for more than a year, you are taxed at long-term rates when you eventually sell your security. A holding period of less than one year results in your transaction being taxed at short-term or ordinary income rates.

Futures contacts are taxed at a blended rate, with 60% of the gain or loss getting long-term capital treatment and 40% getting short-term capital treatment.

It is anticipated that single stock futures will be taxed in a different manner. The 60-40 blended capital gains tax rate will apply only to "dealers." This coincides with the tax treatment of security options. For "non-dealer" investors and traders, gains and losses on single stock futures are treated as if the underling security were traded.

Chapter 8

Sorting Out The Details

Several key issues were raised and had to be solved as a result of the passage of the CFMA, the legislation that allowed single stock futures to begin trading. Many issues were not resolved by August 21, 2001, the official start date trading of single stock futures and the Securities and Exchange Commission and the Commodities Futures Trading Commission had to issue temporary exemptions as they hadn't finalized the rules. Ironically, trading didn't begin as the exchanges themselves were still installing the necessary apparatus for trading these products.

It is interesting to examine some of the many issues that did arise out of the passage of the Commodities Futures Modernization Act of 2000 as it related to single stock futures. Many of the questions raised on the securities-law side of the equation but are nevertheless interesting.

Best Execution

At the time of publication of this book, best execution rules have not been determined but the following is a discussion of its components.

In deciding how to execute orders, your broker has a duty to seek the best execution that is reasonably available for its customers' orders. This means that your broker must evaluate the orders it receives from all customers in the aggregate and periodically assess which competing markets, market makers, or electronic communications networks Electronic Communications Networks (ECN's) offer the most favorable terms of execution. Some of the factors a broker needs to consider when executing its customers' orders for best execution include: the opportunity to get a better price than what is currently quoted, the speed of execution, and the likelihood that the trade will be executed.

Best execution ensures integrity to investors and traders because it makes sure that brokers will act in their customers' best interest when they route and execute orders. It reinforces competition by rewarding those markets that improve their execution quality, and punishes those that don't.

With single stock futures now being available through a broker-dealer who was subject to the best execution rules, questions arose as to the determination of which competing marketplace had the best bid and offer for a market for any given single stock futures.

Perhaps this illustration will make clear the difficulty of deciding where the best market lies.

Let's say you wanted to buy a single stock future on Microsoft and it was trading on seven different exchanges. However, not all the specifications for that contract were identical on each exchange. Let's say three exchanges offered a cash-settled contract, and four settled the contract with the physical delivery of the stock certificate. In addition, let us assume that the settlement dates on each exchange were different. One settled on the third Friday of the delivery month and one settled on the second Tuesday. If all the specifications were the same for each and every contract in terms of size of the contract, delivery date, settlement procedure etc. it would be easy. So, it is clear to see that a broker-dealer or a Futures Commission merchant has quite a problem executing the order quickly at the best prevailing price according to the specific delivery date required. They would have to check all of the competing markets offering identical features that the purchaser of the single stock futures contract wanted. Then, place the order at that exchange and hope that the best bid and offer hadn't changed by time they placed the order. The efficient execution of these orders assumes that information is quickly available for the order routing systems of the various brokers. The more variables in the contracts, the greater the difficulty in execution. Plus, the customer has to be able to specify exactly what he needs. Not all apples are the same. Fortunately, there a only a handful of possible varieties of the same contract for a given single stock future.

Another problem is that the contracts may not be fungible. This means that, even if the identical single stock futures contract is traded in two exchanges, you could not buy it at one exchange and sell it at another at a later date to close out the position.

Say you bought a futures contract for Microsoft at exchange X for 60.50. The next day you wanted to sell it. You would have to sell it on exchange X in order to close out the position even though, theoretically, exchange Y had a better bid. Normally, arbitrageurs would quickly move in but the lack of fungibility makes this difficult though not impossible.

Once a standardized contract is settled and fungibility is allowed, these problems will simply default to where the best bid and offer exist.

Electronic order routing systems at brokerage firms are normally set up to seek the best price for any given security at the moment the order is placed. One hundred shares of Microsoft is one hundred shares of Microsoft no matter how you cut it. One variable, price, makes it a lot easier to decide where the order execution should take place. Each extra variable adds to the difficulty of finding where the trade should take place.

Easier said than done but as single stock futures become more embedded in the investment landscape, this problem will have been worked out by the exchanges and the marketplace.

Beneficial Interest In Securities

For broker-dealers who are subject to federal securities laws, a question arose as to what the net effect of owning single stock futures would be on their customers reported positions. In other words, does a single stock futures position count as being long or short the underlying security?

If a person who owned a single stock futures contract on Microsoft wanted to sell 100 shares of Microsoft, would they be considered exempt from the short sales rule? Will that person have to abide by the up tick rule which requires shorting a stock only on an uptick or a zero-plus tick? Or, would they be considered long the stock by virtue of being in a contract to receive delivery of the stock at the settlement date of the contract?

Basically, all of the questions here revolved around whether of not a position in single stock futures constituted ownership of the underlying security.

Another question that arose pertained to shareholder reporting rules. The government requires that a person holding more than 10% of a security report that position periodically to the Securities and Exchange Commission. In addition to owning the security, would owning single stock futures on that security also constitute ownership of the stock and thus be considered as part of that person's net position that would have to be reported to the government if it exceeded the threshold for required filing? Should that single stock futures position be treated as a long call position and treated in the same manner?

What about tender offers? Can a person be deemed to be long or short the actual security if they are just long or short the single stock futures contract and have not taken physical possession, or required to deliver the underlying security yet because the settlement date of the contract has not occurred? Can they tender based on this position in the futures market even if the contract settles within the tender offer dates?

It should be remembered that a single stock futures contract does not give the owner the right to receive the underlying security until the settlement date, and conversely the seller of the contract doesn't have to deliver the underlying security until the settlement date. In other words, there is no option for early delivery just because you own a single stock futures contract. American-style securities options offer this feature. Security futures contracts are more like European-style contracts that allow exercise only at a given date and not before that date has arrived.

Cash-settled futures securities contracts do not result in delivery of the underlying security but are settled in cash at the expiration of the contract or settlement date.

However, where there is a physical delivery of the securities contract, many of these questions would be appropriate and need clarification.

More than likely, present securities laws will have to be amended to treat the various questions that have arisen because of the legalization and trading of single stock futures contracts and their application to existing federal securities laws.

Anti-fraud and Anti-Manipulation Issues

One of the big considerations for allowing the creation of single stock futures trading was that they were not given a competitive advantage over any other trading vehicle, like options or securities. Everyone wanted to make sure that there wasn't significant incentive to use one vehicle or the other and thus place one product at a competitive disadvantage.

Because certain shareholders, directors and officers of public companies have to make periodic reports about the short-term swing profits and short sales in trading derivatives, the question arose as to what the impact of trading single stock futures on the reporting of these profits would be. What the options industry didn't want was for a loop-hole to be generated that would allow those required to make these reports not have to be subject to the reporting rules if they used single stock futures rather than listed options in their own security

In the most direct terms, it was feared that single stock futures would be not be treated as a derivatives product and subject to the same rules. Many of the concerns were strictly about keeping everything at parity as far as the rules go.

During periods of stock distribution, rules apply to the trading of options and other security derivatives. Would single stock futures also be included in that definition?

Again, the desire was that there also be the same treatment of these instruments. The rules governed cases where a company was in distribution of their own stock or related instrument and how transactions by corporate insiders would be treated or exempted.

Would the same rules apply? If exemptions were granted, then the same exemptions would have to been granted to single stock futures as well.

Would the rules that apply to tender offers and share re-purchase periods be the same for all tradeable instruments? A company often tenders for it's own stock in order to reduce the number of shares outstanding and when they also think that the purchase of their own securities offer a better return than alternative investments. It is during this period that certain transactions in options are subject to the promulgated rules. Again, the desire was for all instruments to be treated in the same manner so as not to generate an unfair advantage to any other instrument.

It is clear from the above discussion that everyone in the trading industry is concerned that their competitors not receive any advantage because of an interpretation of the existing securities laws. Not an unreasonable request because it then puts the onus on the exchanges to offer the best execution and depth of markets for similar, if not identical, trading products. The marketplace would be allowed to decide which product would thrive and which would fall away and not have those decisions tilted to the advantage of one trading instrument because of how existing federal securities rule were written. The investing public and professional financial industry would be able to vote with their trading transactions based on competitive features of the exchanges offering the products and not on the basis of government rules unequally applied to all derivative product. That's what competition on a level playing field is all about.

Carrying Security Futures Positions

Brokerage firms that are both Broker-Dealers (B-D's) and Futures Commission Merchants (FCM's) will have to give their customers the option of placing a single stock futures position in securities account or a commodities account. Each account carries with it different types of protection and recourse in the event of the firm's failure.

Securities accounts held at brokerage accounts are protected by the Securities Investor Protection Corporation (SIPC). When a brokerage is closed due to bankruptcy or other financial difficulties, the Securities Investor Protection Corporation steps in as quickly as possible and within certain limits, works to return cash, stock and other securities held at the firm. Without SIPC, investors at financially troubled brokerage firms might lose their securities or money forever or wait for years while their assets are tied up in court.

However, if the single stock futures position in held in a commodities account at the firm, different rules apply for the protection of customer assets in that account. It would be implicit that the customer waives the protection provided by SIPC and would be subject to the rules established the commodity brokers liquidation procedures of the Bankruptcy Code and certain Commodities Futures Trading Commission rules.

Basically, the customer would have to be informed of the protection and recovery procedures that each of the accounts offers.

There was also talk of creating an account that would allow for cross-margining, netting and related arrangements between futures and securities accounts that fell under the rules for harmonized account maintenance, record keeping and related requirements under the Securities Exchange Act instead of keeping separate accounts for futures transactions and strictly securities transactions.

A lot of confusion could exist when a customer places an order and then must decide where to place the position based upon an understanding of the differences between the protection and recovery afforded by each type of account. The customer, though getting information in writing from his broker, would still be required assess the differences between these two accounts and which one fit his personal, financial requirements.

Joint jurisdiction by both the Securities and Exchange Commission and the Commodities Futures Trading Commission presents brokerage firms that are dually registered as both a Broker-Dealer (BD) and a Futures Commission Merchant (FCM) with complicated bookkeeping decisions that must be represented to the investor or trader. Eventually uniform rules for liquidation of brokerage firms be they strictly a firm dealing in securities or commodities or both will have to be worked out in order to reduce possible confusion to investors.

Dissemination of Quotes

Here's another nightmare to be resolved before trading can begin.

Price reporting is broadcast by each exchange for the products they trade. Usually, the prices are transmitted nearly instantly as they occur through an electronic network that is accessed by quote vendors. A customer can punch in the symbol for a security that he is interested in viewing and see the price that it is trading for almost as fast as the trade occurs. He can also view it on a ticker in a brokerage office. It is an easy procedure because all tradable instruments are assigned a symbol that is standardized for all quote systems. It's the same symbol no matter which quote vendor you use.

What symbol should a single stock futures contract that is traded on five different exchanges have in order not to confuse the public? Let's take Microsoft as an example. The symbol for the security is MSFT. A single stock futures contract for Microsoft trading at OneChicago would have one unique symbol and the identical contract trading on a foreign exchange like LIFFE would have to be assigned a different symbol.

So, it is possible for a customer to call up and ask for a quote on a single stock future on Microsoft and have to wait while his broker looked up the symbol at each of the exchanges where the contract was trading.

When options on single stock futures become available in 2003, the nightmare begins all over again, and with a vengeance. As options have many, many price points as well as possible months. Each would require a symbol that would identify the exact strike price, month and the exchange where the option traded. This means that potentially an unimaginable amount of symbols would have to be allocated to each and every series.

With a potential universe of more than 1,500 securities available currently, it is easy to recognize the scope of this massive undertaking.

Conflicts existed between futures exchanges and securities exchanges over symbol overlaps. The symbol on a futures exchange might represent one commodity and that same symbol on an exchange might represent a security. The task was to eliminate these conflicts. A task force was created from the ranks of market data vendors, brokerage firms and the exchanges to resolve this problem so that this information could easily be used in existing order entry systems, back office order processing operations, and market data vendors systems.

As you can see, this was a vast undertaking that required gigantic cooperation among the various segments of the financial community.

The public only sees a smooth running, efficient order processing and reporting operation but never really gets to see the monumental tasks and elements that have to be in place to give this appearance. Each and every tiny piece creates even more coordination and cooperation between the industry components. No easy task and very, very time consuming.

All of these endless details had to be resolved so that price dissemination would be efficient and that decision making by investors and traders would be facilitated. And, miraculously, they have been resolved so that trading will prove to be an efficient operation.

Margin requirements

Since futures exchanges have traditionally set the margin requirements (performance bonds) at a small percentage of the contract's total value, this was one of the most watched and protected areas. Unlike securities, no other monies are initially involved until either the performance bond requirements change or the account has dropped below the maintenance requirements. There is no unpaid balance and therefore no interest charged.

Normally, on a New York Stock Exchange traded security, an investor trading on margin would have to put up at least 50% of the value of the underlying security and pay interest on the balance to his broker at the going call margin rate.

For instance, the purchase of 100 shares of Microsoft trading at $60 a share would require a margin deposit of half of the value of the total purchase, or $3,000 per 100 shares bought and the balance of $3,000 could be borrowed from his broker.

So, it was obvious to all that if futures exchanges were allowed to set the performance bonds at the traditional rates of 5-10% of the value of the total contact value, they would definitely enjoy a strong competitive advantage. Under traditional performance bond requirements, the futures exchanges could have set the performance bond requirement for the single stock futures contract on Microsoft shares at, say 10% of the value of the contract. That would mean that only $600 per contract would have to be deposited as a performance bond while the Federal Reserve requirement under Regulation T would have been $3,000 for 100 shares purchased on the NYSE. Obviously, that wasn't going to fly.

So, how would this disparity be resolved? Since one could create an synthetic single stock futures position using a combination of long call/short puts options or long put/short call options if they wanted to go through the trouble, the margin rules that would govern that position would be the minimum performance bond allowed. This would level the playing field between the competing exchanges for trading dollars, at least in terms of margin requirements (performance bonds on futures exchanges).

Another point to be considered was how to calculate the single stock futures' holders other cash and options position figures in the required margin requirements.

Perhaps the most controversial aspect of all the margin rules (performance bond requirements) relates to who will ultimately have the final authority over this important and competitive aspect of this business, self-regulated organizations, the Commodities Futures Trading Commission (CFTC), the Securities and Exchange Commission (SEC), or even the Federal Reserve Bank. As the market develops and trading history evolves, the decision and rationale for which should govern will be determined.

Floor-Trading Rules

Exchanges impose rules on the trading of their own members. They are not uniform and possibly could create an unfair advantage for members of one exchange at the expense of others. Also, trading in single stock futures on notice-registered exchanges are not under the same rules at trading in security futures in non-notice registered exchanges. Notice registered exchanges operate under rules spelled out under the Commodities Exchange Act.

The fear was that the rules might create unfair advantages to members and it was desired that the rules be examined so that the playing field would remain level for all players.

Registration of Market Makers

One of the rules that needed to be dealt with was to how to allow Futures Commissions Merchants to place orders on securities exchanges that list and trade single stock futures.

To expedite this, it was agreed that they would be allowed to notice-register as broker dealers for the limited purpose of effecting single stock futures trades.

Suitability Rules

The suitability rules for customers of Futures Commissions Merchants would have to conform to more closely the sales practice code of the NASD as a condition for notice registration.

Chapter 9

STATEMENTS & INTERVIEWS

The forces that influenced the legislation that created the Commodities Futures Modernization Act of 2000 that allowed the lifting of the ban on single stock futures were many and varied. They came from a large variety of interested parties and government agencies that worked together to shape the legislation.

The legislators had to juggle competing interests and arrive at a bill that was fair and equitable to all concerned. The seeming conflict between the securities exchanges and futures exchanges had to be addressed as well as the jurisdictional questions of the Securities and Exchange Commission and the Commodities Futures Trading Commission had to be solved as well. Protecting the investing public was another issue that warranted closer attention.

The real catalyst for all of this the fact that if the competing forces didn't resolve all of the issues that had heretofore impeded the lifting of the Shad/Johnson accord was the threat of foreign competition establishing too strong a first-mover advantage and thus establishing the market for single stock futures on foreign shores. This threat helped to resolve the differences and pull together that the largest marketplace in the world for equities would also be the home of the largest marketplace in the world for single stock futures.

Here are quotes from some of the leading contributors to this important and historic legislation:

From The Exchanges

"The futures industry would be prepared to embrace the equivalent margin structure as the Chicago Board Options Exchange. So that fictitious objection has no currency anymore."
—Leo Melamed Chairman Emeritus of the Chicago Mercantile Exchange, Derivatives Roundtable, published by Institutional Investor Newsletter's web site, wallstreetletter.com, November15,1999

***

"Why are the agricultural people involved at all? They are the most pampered lobby of all. There are more agricultural economists than there are farmers!"
—Merton Miller Derivatives Roundtable, published by Institutional Investor Newsletter's web site, wallstreetletter.com, November15,1999

***

"Our goal was equivalent regulatory treatment for functionally equivalent trading facilities, clearing houses and intermediaries. We are disappointed that our efforts to create a fair and level playing field have not been heeded."
—Scott Gordon, Chairman, Chicago Mercantile Exchange (CME) Press Release, Februrary 10, 2000

***

"While the Working Group recognizes the regulatory disparities and blurred product distinctions that handcuff U.S. futures exchanges in today's competitive global market, the Report does almost nothing to address those issues,"
—Scott Gordon, Chairman, Chicago Mercantile Exchange (CME) Press Release, Februrary 10, 2000

***

"That temporary ban lasted 18 years during which time single stock futures have thrived in the OTC market in the form of equity swaps, and on option exchanges in the form of synthetic futures."
—Scott Gordon, Chairman, Chicago Mercantile Exchange (CME) Press Release , May 8, 2000

***

"The commission has been both responsible and responsive to the concerns of all elements in the financial services industry. The tone of the CFTC's proposal is consistent with a progressive regulatory philosophy that depends competition among markets..." and demonstrates "...a deepening understanding of the complex technological and competitive issues facing our markets and a commitment to providing much-needed regulatory relief."

—Scott Gordon, Chairman, Chicago Mercantile Exchange (CME) Press Release , May 8, 2000

***

"LIFFE's announcement that it will trade single stock futures on five U.S. securities is the best possible evidence of the unfair competition the U.S. futures exchanges face today. LIFFE will trade in four months a product we are banned by federal statute from trading. For 18 years we have asked to have that ban lifted, but at every turn we have met delay. Those delays have only worked to the advantage of our foreign competitors.

—CME, CBOT Comment on London Exchange Plan to Trade Futures on U.S. Stocks, September 20, 2000

***

"We fully understand the need to protect one's competitive position and the tendency to protect one's turf, but when that behavior affects the best interests of the United States, it is indefensible."

—CME, CBOT Comment on London Exchange Plan to Trade Futures on U.S. Stocks, September 20, 2000

***

"This partnership moves Nasdaq into a market segment which is new but consistent with our global programme. We expect these instruments to become important investment vehicles in the United States and Europe. This transatlantic partnership opens new opportunities for both Nasdaq and Liffe — it gets us to market faster and positions us well to offer state-of-the-art electronic trading to investors in both the U.S. and Europe. We chose LIFFE CONNECT™ because it is the most advanced electronic derivatives trading system in the world, already proven to trade the most complex financial contracts, including Universal trading system."

—Frank G. Zarb, Chairman of Nasdaq, Nasdaq/LIFFE Press Release Stock Futures, March 26, 2001

***

"Anticipating the growth in global equity trading, LIFFE pioneered the development of futures on global stocks with the successful launch of its universal stock futures earlier this year. Our partnership with Nasdaq, a giant in the equity world, enables us to build on the momentum we have already achieved. The strength of Nasdaq's brand and its preeminent position in the US equity market will make our single stock futures offering a compelling choice for both retail and institutional customers in the U.S., as well as in Europe and beyond. As a first step, LIFFE and Nasdaq together are taking the revolution which LIFFE started, to the biggest capital market in the world, the United States of America."

—Brian Williamson, LIFFE's Chairman, Nasdaq/LIFFE Press Release, March 26, 2001

***

"The world is moving rapidly toward electronic trading across a wide array of financial instruments. At the same time, geographic barriers are coming down. This partnership is an important and tangible step in both directions — bringing more products and choices to investors in the United States and Europe."

—John Hilley, Chairman and Chief Executive Officer of Nasdaq International Inc., Nasdaq/LIFFE Press Release, March 26, 2001

***

"Our partnership with Nasdaq represents a significant milestone in realizing LIFFE's ambitions to become a leading provider of electronic market solutions. Nasdaq can be justly proud of its reputation as an innovator and leader in electronic stock market trading. Its choice of LIFFE CONNECT™ is a major endorsement of our trading platform and technology capabilities."

—Hugh Freedberg, Chief Executive LIFFE, Nasdaq/LIFFE Press Release, March 26, 2001

***

"We are very excited about this opportunity at the CBOE and are diligently preparing for launch later this year."

—William J. Brodsky, Chairman and CEO of the CBOE, Remarks to the Investment Analysts Society of Chicago, March 1, 2001

***

"Many of you have customers and investment funds so you really do need to understand the impact of all new investment vehicles and this is as great a development as we've had in a long, long time."
—William J. Brodsky, Chairman and CEO of the CBOE, Remarks to the Investment Analysts Society of Chicago, March 1, 2001

***

"At the CBOE, we not only plan to trade the product we plan to dominate the field."
—William J. Brodsky, Chairman and CEO of the CBOE, Remarks to the Investment Analysts Society of Chicago, March 1, 2001

***

"The bottom line, at least from our perspective, was that we wanted to make sure there was regulatory parity to ensure people wouldn't choose to trade a future on a stock versus an option on a stock purely because of unfair regulatory advantages. I'm also happy to say that what I call the 'investor protection rules' provided a level playing field for both futures and securities exchanges. Fair and concurrent jurisdiction of the SEC and the CFTC was ultimately achieved for the first time."
—William J. Brodsky, Chairman and CEO of the CBOE, Remarks to the Investment Analysts Society of Chicago, March 1, 2001

***

"We'll look at single stock futures as to whether our clients want us to list them."
—A.D. Frazier, CHX President and Chief Executive Officer Reuters, April 26, 2001

***

"Today's announcement highlights the innovation and entrepreneurial spirit among Chicago's exchanges. This exciting new initiative combines the best of securities and futures trading. Our willingness to work together on this venture will ensure that Chicago remains the world's center in derivatives trading and risk management."
—William Brodsky, CBOE Chairman and Chief Executive Officer, CME/CBOE/CBOT Press Release, May 14, 2001

"The creation of this joint venture recognizes the tremendous synergies of CME and CBOE, making us a formidable competitor in the global marketplace for single stock futures. Our complementary customer bases of retail and institutional investors will benefit from the efforts of all three Chicago exchanges to establish deep pools of liquidity in these products."

—*Scott Gordon, CME Chairman,* CME/CBOE/CBOT Press Release, May 14, 2001

***

"Our largest customers have emphasized the importance of collaboration between the CBOE and CME to combine the capabilities, distribution and connectivity of the futures and securities worlds," "This alliance should also provide the highest level of capital efficiency for our customers who trade in both futures and options."

—Jim McNulty, President and Chief Executive Officer, CME, CME/CBOE/CBOT Press Release, May 14, 2001

***

"The CBOT is pleased to work with the leadership of CBOE and CME in this initiative to bring this exciting new product to our markets, The involvement of our members and the access to our customers will make important contributions to the success of this venture. The joint venture will be a for-profit company, will have its own management and board, and will be separately organized as a regulated exchange."

—Nicholas Neubauer, Chairman of the Chicago Board of Trade, CME/CBOE/CBOT Press Release, May 14, 2001

***

One thing should remain clear: the CBOT was never offered more than 10%. "That was all that we offered. The market theoretically could have been launched by the Merc and the CBOE alone. We just felt that [offering the CBOT a minority stake] was the proper thing to do, but there never was any talk about more than 10%."

—Leo Melamed CME Senior Advisor and Chairman Emeritus. Wall Street and Technology July 11, 2001

"Bill Rainer's experience encompasses the worlds of investment, trading and market regulation, and his track record of vision and innovation are ideal for the new CME-CBOE-CBOT joint venture on single stock futures. Bill's knowledge and experience will enable him to hit the ground running in meeting customers' needs for single stock futures."
　　　　—Scott Gordon, Chairman of CME, Chicago Mercantile Exchange Press Release, August 29, 2001

***

"The CBOE-CME-CBOT joint venture is an historic development for Chicago, and it was important to find the right person, capable of meeting the many challenges that lie ahead. Bill Rainer's depth of experience in a multitude of areas, and the leadership he will provide, will be a major asset for the joint venture."
　　　　—William Brodsky, CBOE Chairman and Chief Executive Officer, Chicago Mercantile Exchange Press Release, August 29, 2001

***

"This is an exciting opportunity. Given the unique composition of our ownership, and the depth and quality of resources available to our company, we are positioned to provide a strong marketplace for single stock futures. I am eager to move to Chicago and to get started,"
　　　　—William Rainer, Chicago Mercantile Exchange Press Release, August 29, 2001

***

"The CFTC has put us one giant step closer to offering single stock futures to U.S. investors. We are excited and prepared to be the leader in single stock futures trading and are anticipating considerable interest in this product. Being the first exchange approved by the CFTC only heightens our drive to be the premier U.S. exchange for single stock futures. The CFTC is to be applauded for quickly responding to the needs of the market."
　　　　— Nasdaq/Liffe Markets (NQLX) Press Release interim CEO Bob Fitzsimmons, August 22, 2001

"Our proven track record in derivatives and our experience in trading a wide range of diverse products uniquely positions the American Stock Exchange to be successful with single stock futures."
—Salvatore Sodano, Amex Chairman and CEO, American Stock Exchange Press Release, September 6, 2001

***

"The inherent advantages of Amex's specialist market structure, including the deep liquidity provided by Wall Street's leading firms, will give us a distinct competitive advantage in trading these exciting new products."
—Joseph Stefanelli, Amex Executive Vice President of Derivatives, American Stock Exchange Press Release, September 6, 2001

***

"With SGX single stock futures, institutional and individual investors will have a versatile financial tool to better manage their investments and maximize their profitability by taking advantage of varying market opportunities. The introduction of SINGLE STOCK FUTURES represents a true synergy of our securities and derivatives markets, and we expect to see increased inter-market trading and hedging activities involving these two markets."
—Thomas Kloet, CEO of Singapore Exchange Limited (SGX) Press Release September 25, 2001

***

"I am enthused that Chicago's exchanges have worked so well together to understand and address our customers' needs and our members' concerns. We have designed a product that, I believe, will appeal to our customers, and a business structure that will provide great benefit to our members."
—Mark Duffy, Vice Chairman, CBOE

***

"There is a large community of day traders that will use single stock futures. For them it will be easier. If we can connect in, plug in to that community, we're going to get retail trade of that kind."

"The institutional user has found—those same people that run around years ago worrying what futures were going to do to the New York Stock Exchange trading, today walk on the New York Stock Exchange floor, look at monitors everywhere on that floor to see what are the futures prices saying."
—Leo Melamed, chairman and CEO of Melamed & Associates and Chairman emeritus and senior policy advisor of the Chicago Mercantile Exchange, The Merton Miller Group, Reston Va, as reported in Wallstreetletter.com

From The Firms

"There are about 20-21 million people trading equities out there. That's a natural audience for this."
  —Joseph Murphy, CEO Refco Global Futures, Businessweek Online, February 26, 2001

***

"As a result of this legislation, the American investor will soon be able to realize the potential for increased benefits by trading stock futures and stock options."
  —Paul Finnegan, Vice President Marketing/Business Development Man Financial Inc., PRNewswire, April 2, 2001

***

"We've been able to see two government agencies who have butted heads several times work together to make this agreement and help U.S. exchanges remain competitive."
  —Steve Greenberg, President of Alaron Trading Corp. Futures Magazine April 2001

***

"Any European market that tries to attack the U.S. SINGLE STOCK FUTURE market on its own is taking a big risk. The cost of entry is much higher nowadays than it used to be in the past... and I think for any foreign exchange to try some type of an entree into the U.S. without a domestic partner would be foolhardy."
  —Leslie Rosenthal A managing partner at Rosenthal Collins Group. Wall Street and Technology July 11, 2001

***

"Rather than forming an alliance, a foreign market may want to consider buying an existing, for-profit exchange outright. They can't come in here on their own. It would be like the CBOT deciding they're going to start up business in London and capture the market."
  —Michael Manning, President and CEO Rand Financial Services, Wall Street and Technology July 11, 2001

"Let me run through or share with you at least the English experience with single stock futures, which has the grandiose history of five days, but does have two years of study. We found in two years of study that it's far cheaper. You have to bear in mind that with options, if you're going to create a synthetic future, you have to do two things. You have to get long a put, short a call or visa versa to create it. You've got two bid/ask spreads and two commissions. So, you've got twice the bid ask spreads, so you've got big transaction costs."
—Richard Sandor, chairman of Environmental Financial Products, The Merton Miller Group, Reston Va, as reported in Wallstreetletter.com

FROM CONGRESSIONAL TESTIMONY

"I understand what frozen pork belly contracts do. They serve an economic purpose. I don't get it with reference to individual stocks."

"I think what I have been trying to argue is there is no economic purpose."
—Statement of James L. Cochrane, Senior Vice-President, Strategy and Planning and Chief Economist, New York Stock Exchange, Inc., Reauthorization of the Commodity Futures Trading commission, May 20, 1999

***

"It appears that the United States is somewhat reluctant to adapt market forces to a market to be able to remain in the leadership role that it is in."
—Representative Baldacci of Maine, reauthorization of the commodity futures trading commission subcommittee on Risk Management, Research, and Specialty Crops, Committee on Agriculture, MAY 20, 1999

***

"The statutory restrictions on securities-based derivatives, known as the Shad-Johnson Accord, should be lifted so that futures exchanges and OTC markets may offer those innovative products just as they are all over the world. The current ban was enacted 18 years ago as a "temporary foreclosure" while the agencies studied the issues. Eighteen years is "temporary" enough. Congress must open this area to full competition as well."
—Testimony of David P. Brennan Chairman of the Board of Directors Board of Trade of the City of Chicago, Before the Subcommittee on Research, Nutrition, and General Legislation, of the Senate Agriculture Committee March 20, 2000

"The ban on single securities futures should be lifted. Free and fair competition should be allowed. That will make the markets stronger and lead to more efficient risk management for securities market participants."
—Testimony of David P. Brennan Chairman of the Board of Directors Board of Trade of the City of Chicago, Before the Subcommittee on Research, Nutrition, and General Legislation, of the Senate Agriculture Committee March 20, 2000

***

"We are less sanguine aabout reform of the Shad/Johnson Accord. Eighteen years ago the Shad/Johnson Accord divided jurisdiction between the SEC and CFTC and included a temorary ban on most eequity futures contracts. That temporary ban lasted 18 years during which time single stock futures have thrived in the OTC market in the form of equity swaps and on option exchanges in the form of synthetic futures. Recently the President's Working Group and congressional leaders called for an end to the ban."
—Testimony of McNulty Before Senate Agriculture Committee March 20, 2000

***

"The dominance of U.S. futures exchanges has eroded. Their ability to compete with the over-the-counter market and foreign exchanges has been hampered by U.S. regulatory policy."
—Testimony of McNulty Before Senate Agriculture Committee March 20, 2000

***

"London profited from the restrictive policies in the USA, which reinforced London's comparative advantage as a benign location."
—Testimony of McNulty Before Senate Agriculture Committee March 20, 2000

***

"Shad-Johnson is being used as a weapon against competition."
—Testimony of McNulty Before Senate Agriculture Committee March 20, 2000

"The stock exchanges prefer less competition; but if competition breaks out they prefer to trade the instruments themselves."
—Testimony of McNulty Before Senate Agriculture Committee March 20, 2000

***

"Futures trading of equity indices has enhanced customer opportunity with none of the ill consequences predicted by the SEC or securities exchanges. In fact, their business has directly benefited."
—Testimony of McNulty Before Senate Agriculture Committee March 20, 2000

***

"The most important issue to Merrill Lynch relating to these markets is legal certainty. The firm and its customers must be confident that they understand the requirements applied to the transactions they enter into, the systems they use, and the counter parties with which they deal. Those requirements must be clear and not subject to change based upon philosophical changes at the regulator. And most importantly, a failure to adhere to a specific regulatory requirement should not, except in extraordinary circumstances, result in the "death penalty" - allowing a counter party on the losing side of a transaction to walk away from its obligations under the guise of an illegality defense."
—Testimony of Peter Lee, Managing Director, Merrill Lynch Futures before U.S. Senate Committee on Agriculture, Nutrition & Forestry, March 20, 2000

***

"Our customers want to trade more stock index contracts on foreign exchanges. And they want the opportunity to trade individual stock futures contracts on U.S. exchanges. The Shad-Johnson Accord restricts U.S. customers from accessing some of the most rapidly growing exchange traded contracts globally. U.S. futures exchanges are now disadvantaged because the SEC has been more restrictive in approving stock index futures contracts trading on futures exchanges than index contracts traded on securities exchanges. This puts futures exchanges at a disadvantage. Our customers want broader access to all forms of equity contracts wherever they trade."
—Testimony of Jan R. Waye, Senior Vice President, Cargill Investor Services, Inc before   U.S. Senate Committee on Agriculture, Nutrition & Forestry, March 20, 2000

"My real point is that the burgeoning number of exchanges and the corresponding changes to the entire industry, including its self-regulatory structure, point out the need for action now."
—Testimony of Robert K. Wilmouth, President, National Futures Association, Inc before U.S. Senate Committee on Agriculture, Nutrition & Forestry, March 20, 2000

***

"The proposed framework is intended to promote innovation, maintain U.S. competitiveness, reduce systemic risk, and protect derivatives customers. Any proposal ultimately adopted will not be tailored to the desires of any special interest or driven by jurisdictional concerns. We want to find solutions that serve the public interest."
—Testimony of C. Robert Paul, General Counsel, Commodity Futures Trading Commission before U.S. Senate Committee on Agriculture, Nutrition & Forestry, March 20, 2000

***

"We contend that the goal of efficient market places where all market participants compete on a level playing field can be achieved cheaply and easily with available technology. The only thing that has stymied its implementation in the past has been the intentional acts by the economically advantaged groups to cripple the potential of the systems."
—Testimony of David Downey Executive Vice President, Interactive Brokers LLC before U.S. Senate Committee on Agriculture, Nutrition & Forestry, March 20, 2000

***

"I strongly believe that the Senate Banking Committee should not allow the perpetuation of anti-competitive, unequal regulation in equity products by permitting single stock futures without submitting the product to equivalent securities regulation."
—Testimony of William J. Brodsky Chairman and Chief Executive Officer Chicago Board Options Exchange, "Maintaining Leadership in the Financial Marketplace of the Future" before the Senate Banking Committee May 8, 2000

"We are the only major country in the world that does not have a Single regulatory body that oversees all equity products. I recognize that a merger of the SEC and CFTC would be difficult to accomplish, but it is long overdue."
—Testimony of William J. Brodsky Chairman and Chief Executive Officer Chicago Board Options Exchange, "Maintaining Leadership in the Financial Marketplace of the Future" before the Senate Banking Committee May 8, 2000

***

"In order to meet today's global challenges, we need to bring products to market quickly and make rule changes promptly."
—Testimony of William J. Brodsky Chairman and Chief Executive Officer Chicago Board Options Exchange, "Maintaining Leadership in the Financial Marketplace of the Future" before the Senate Banking Committee May 8, 2000

From Regulatory Agencies

"If we as regulators fail to provide the right services at the right price <u>now</u>, the regulated industry will not be able to compete, business will flow overseas or to OTC markets, and we will have little or nothing left to regulate."
—Robert K. Wilmouth, President, National Futures Association befor the Commodity Futures Trading Commission, June 27, 2000

***

"S. 2697 would reauthorize funding for the activities of the Commodity Futures Trading Commission (CFTC) during the 2001-2005 period. The bill would also allow the trading of single stock futures under certain conditions, with oversight being shared by the CFTC and the Securities and Exchange Commission (SEC). In addition, S. 2697 would clarify that certain over-the-counter derivative transactions are outside of the jurisdiction of the CFTC. The bill also would authorize the CFTC to designate boards of trade as contract markets or execution facilities for derivatives transactions. Assuming appropriation of the necessary amounts, CBO estimates that implementing this legislation would cost $363 million over the 2001-2005 period."
—Congressional Budget Office Cost Estimate for S. 2697 Commodity Futures Modernization Act of 2000. July 11, 2000

"Our members agree generally that significant benefits would likely accrue to market participants who were able to implement risk management and investment decisions by using single stock futures and futures on narrowly defined equity indices."

"We are pleased to enclose the agreement reached between the CFTC and SEC to permit the trading of single stock futures and narrow-based stock indices."

—Transmittal Letters Re: SEC/CFTC Agreement to Lift Ban on Single Stock Futures. Lawrence H. Summers Secretary, Department of the Treasury, Arthur Levitt, Chairman Securities and Exchange Commission, Alan Greenspan, Chairman Board of Governors of the Federal Reserve, William J. Rainer, Chairman, Commodity Futures Trading Commission. September 14, 2000

***

"Unless our laws and regulations relating to OTC derivatives are modernized, we run the risk that innovation will be stifled, depriving the American economy of the benefits that the derivatives markets can provide, and hampering the efforts of our financial markets and businesses to compete globally."

—Transmittal Letters Re: SEC/CFTC Agreement to Lift Ban on Single Stock Futures. Lawrence H. Summers Secretary, Department of the Treasury, Arthur Levitt, Chairman Securities and Exchange Commission, Alan Greenspan, Chairman Board of Governors of the Federal Reserve, William J. Rainer, Chairman, Commodity Futures Trading Commission. September 14, 2000

***

"It is my goal to ensure that these products trade free from unnecessary or duplicative regulation and I believe that today's rules serve to further accomplish that goal."

—Acting Chairman James E. Newsome CCH no.651 August 23, 2001

From Industry Associations

"Our members agree generally that significant benefits would likely accrue to market participants who were able to implement risk management and investment decisions by using single stock futures and futures on narrowly defined equity indices."

    —William P. Miller, Senior Vice President and Independent Risk officer of Commonfund, Statement of the End-Users of Derivatives Council of the Association for Financial Professionals before the U.S. House of Representative, Committee on Agriculture, Subcommittee on Risk Management, Research and Specialty Crops. February 15, 2000

***

"While SIA shares the view of the President's Working Group Report that single stock (or narrow-based equity) futures should not be prohibited by law, these products should not be permitted to trade without first ensuring that an appropriate regulatory infrastructure is in place."

    —Marc E. Lackritz, President, Securities Industry Association Press Release, June 9, 2000

***

"We are encouraged by the cooperation we have seen between the CFTC and SEC on this issue. The final rules, as revised, will go a long way in assuring the success of these products."

    — Damgard. August 22, 2001 Futures Industry Association Press Release

***

"The Managed Funds Association (MFA) strongly supports Congress's efforts to modernize the Commodity Exchange Act and reauthorize the Commodity Futures Trading Commission."

    —Comment Letter to the CFTC, from the Managed Funds Association, John G. Gaine, President

***

" Single stock futures are currently available in many developed markets. Not allowing U.S. markets to offer and trade similar contracts places U.S. markets, as well as U.S. participants in those markets, at considerable competitive disadvantage vis-à-vis their international counterparts."

    —Comment Letter to the CFTC, From The Derivatives Subcommittee of the Association for Investment Management and Research's (AIMR) Advocacy Advisory Committee, Gary L. Gastineau, Maria J. A

Chapter 10

Summary

The mix of trading instruments that affect the pricing of single stock futures, options on stocks and their underlying equity are important variables in the equation that affects the price of any security.

PART ONE gives the reader a basic education in the components of instruments affecting pricing decisions.

PART TWO presents an in-depth look at single stock futures, how they will be traded, various strategies, and how options and the price of the security being traded affect each other.

PART THREE is a brief history with commentary about the creation of single stock futures.

The major difference between a security and its derivatives is that the security confers ownership and its derivatives (options and futures) do not. Options allow one to limit risk but require a payment (premium) for this protection. The stock has to move enough to recapture the premium and yield a profit.

Single stock futures (single stock futures) will allow the trader the opportunity to capture the price move in a given stock with lower financial requirements than the purchase of the underlying security whether on margin or paid for in full. They closely parallel the price movement of the equity. Plus, there is no interest charged on the difference between the actual value of the future and the deposit (performance bond). Shorting a single stock futures does not require an uptick as with listed securities making it easier to make this kind of transaction at any given moment.

The future of single stock futures is still being written but promises to be an innovation whose time has come. Given the size of the equities markets and the many advantages of trading single stock futures, it won't be long before equity traders add them to their arsenal of trading instruments. The trading world is awaiting the marketplace's verdict with great eagerness.

Chapter 11

QUESTIONS AND ANSWERS

Q. How long will it take for a deep, liquid market to develop in single stock futures?

A. Often, it takes between 12-18 months for a new market to develop. But because of the track record and proven history of stock index futures and options, it could be a lot shorter.

Q. When will options on single stock futures be allowed to trade?

A. Not until 2003.

Q. What is one of the biggest differences between trading single stock futures and trading the underling security?

A. Single stock futures will give the trader better leverage than trading the underlying stock. Margin requirements (performance bonds in futures) are much higher for securities than they will be for single stock futures. Stocks are usually margined at 50% of the total price of the stock whereas single stock futures will probably require a minimum deposit equal to the value of the contract.

Q. What about the short sale rule?

A. There is no short sale rule in trading futures. You simply hit the bid and you have established your short position. Stocks

147

require an uptick (higher price than the previous sale) before you can establish a short position. You can always sell out your long positions at the bid but must wait until there is an uptick or zero-plus tick before you can sell stock short.

Q. Who sets margin or performance bond requirements?

A. The Federal Reserve Bank sets margin rates and will do so for initially for single stock futures. The exchanges and brokerage firms can set higher requirements if they feel it necessary. Normally, performance bond requirements are set by the futures exchanges and not a government agency. However, since this is the launching of a new trading product that is closely related to the underlying security, it was decided that the Federal Reserve Bank should have input. Brokerage firms can also impose higher requirements.

Q. Will there be position limits?

A. No, there will not be any position limits (the number of contracts any one individual or entity can own) but there will be position-reporting requirements. If an entity controls more than 200 contracts of a single stock futures contract, they must file a position report to the appropriate authority?

Q. Is it possible for there to be more contracts sold than the number of shares that exist for the underlying security?

A. Theoretically, yes. However, it is doubtful that anyone could accumulate that big a position. Most companies have millions of shares outstanding. It is highly unlikely that the open-interest in any given single stock futures contract will exceed the outstanding shares in the underlying security.

Q. Will the contract specifications be identical on all of the exchanges competing for single stock futures business?

A. They might be the same but they will not be fungible. This means that the same single stock futures contract purchased on one exchange and sold on another do not offset each other. In other words, you will be carrying positions on two different exchanges and have to close out the position on the exchange where you initiated the trade. Of course, this could change as the product develops market acceptance.

Q. How will the buy and sell orders be matched?

A. Depends on the exchange. The new joint venture, OneChicago, has an order-matching engine that will electronically match all bids and offers. Some exchanges will have a combination of electronic execution and open-outcry system for matching buyers and sellers.

Q. How many exchanges will be offering single stock futures?

A. In the United States, four for sure. OneChicago, the NASDAQ/LIFFE (NQLX) partnership, American Stock Exchange and Islands. As demand for this product develops, others will be sure to follow.

Other ECN's and other stock exchanges will be certain to jump in after the pioneering effort of the other exchanges pans out. They will certainly be offering single stock futures contracts on the same stocks. The game will go to the exchange offering the most liquidity and cheapest execution costs. Competition will certainly help drive down the costs of doing business at the competing exchanges.

Q. Do you have to open a futures trading account to trade these single stock futures?

A. No, you can trade them either at a securities firm in your regular stock account or in your futures account at a firm that deals exclusively in futures contracts. You should check with your broker for the specific ramifications of trading these instruments in your securities account or your futures account at that firm.

Q. Who will help provide the liquidity for these instruments at the onset of trading?

A. Certain exchanges will use designated market makers who will provide bids and offers. These market makers will be rewarded on a per contract executed basis. As these markets develop, the marketplace will develop it's own liquidity and the designated primary market makers (DPM's), as they are called, will be phased out and the order books will be filled in by the myriad of market participants. Other exchanges will have to devise incentive plans in order to develop the liquidity that traders seek in active markets. DPM's have an obligation to provide a continuous two sided market and in turn may receive orderflow privileges.

Q. How many stocks will be listed initially?

A. At first, just the most active, highly traded stocks will be listed. It should be noted that when the CBOE started, they listed a handful of companies and now offer options on more than 1,500 companies. Obviously, if there is demand for this product, the listings will follow.

Q. What about foreign exchanges?

A. Foreign exchanges have been trading single stock futures for some time now. Most list domestic companies but two,

LIFFE and Hong Kong, are offering single stock futures on a few American companies. This move by these foreign exchanges hastened the lifting of the ban on single stock futures in the United States.

Q. Why haven't single stock futures been successful on foreign exchanges that have been trading them for years?

A. It really comes down to marketing muscle. The exchanges in the United States have the ability to promote their products plus the US is the largest equity market place in the world.

Q. What's going to make them popular here?

A. Stock index futures have paved the way for security futures products. They have been an enormously popular trading and investing tool used by every level of the trading and investing community. The similarities between the two products augurs well for their success. Leverage and the ability to effect short sales puts them at a significant advantage over stocks for those interested in capturing just price movement. Other than the initial performance bond (margin), no other money is required and no interest is charged on the difference between the total value of the contract and the amount of the performance bond. Stocks purchased on margin require the buyer to pay interest on the difference between the margin deposit and the total purchase price.

Q. Will they be cash-settled like index products?

A. Not at the NQLX, AMEX, Island and OneChicago. If the contracts are not closed out before the expiration of the contract month, the seller will have to deliver the underlying certificate and the buyer will have to pay the balance due. Given these conditions, it is very likely that most contracts will be closed out before their expiration. Stock index contracts are automatically closed (cash-settled at expiration) if the holders should decide not to close them out before expiration. Their accounts are either debited or credited by the positive or negative difference in price movement that has occurred since initiation of their position.

Q. Why is the contract size so small?

A. Initially, the contract will cover 100 shares of the underlying security. Almost all listed stock options contracts are for 100 shares of stock. This overlay will allow for a greater amount of arbitrage between the stock, the option and the single stock futures contract as they cover the same number of shares.

Q. Will the contract size be increased so that the product will be more attractive to institutional investors?

A. If customer demand warrants, it will be considered by the exchanges. Because institutional traders carry much larger positions and are very conscious of execution costs. To hedge a position of 20,000 shares would require 200 contracts at the 100 share contract size. However, a contract size of 1,000 shares would only require 20 contracts to cover the position. Plus, the costs associated with putting on that position, would be significantly lower.

Q. Why is the performance bond lower than the margin requirements for the underlying stock?

A. Traditionally, futures contract performance bonds have usually been in the range of 5% to 15% of the total value of the contract. Because single stock futures contracts are not identical to the underlying security (they do not give the holder ownership rights or entitle them to dividends) they are treated differently in terms of performance bond (margin) requirements. It should be kept in mind, that the individual firms can raise their own performance requirements if necessary and the performance bonds are the minimum required.

Glossary of Futures, Options and Securities Terms

This is an extensive and mixed glossary because the language of futures, options and securities is unique and varied. There are more words here than the average person who will be trading single stock futures needs to know but these have been made available for anyone interested in exploring this subject in more depth.

A

ACTUALS: An actual physical commodity someone is buying or selling, e.g., pork bellies, cattle, soybeans, corn, gold, silver, Treasury bonds, Euro-bonds etc.

AMERICAN-STYLE OPTION: An option contract that may be exercised at any time between the date of purchase and the expiration date. Most exchange-traded options are American-style positions. Also referred to as "against actuals" or "versus cash."

ARBITRAGE: The simultaneous purchase and sale of similar commodities or securities instruments in different markets to take advantage of price discrepancies.

ARBITRATION: A procedure of settling disputes between members, or between members and customers.

ASSIGN: To make an option seller perform his obligation to assume a short futures position (as a seller of a call option) or a long futures position (as a seller of a put option).

ASSOCIATED PERSON (AP): Individual who solicits orders, customers, or customer funds (or who supervises persons performing such duties) on behalf of a Futures Commission Merchant, an Introducing Broker, a Commodity Trading Adviser, or a Commodity Pool Operator.

AT-THE-MONEY OPTION: An option with a strike price that is equal, or approximately equal, to the current market price of the underlying futures contract or security.

B

BAR CHART: A chart that graphs the high, low, and settlement prices for a specific trading session over a certain period of time.

BASIS: The difference between the current cash price and the futures price of the same commodity. Unless otherwise specified, the price of the nearby futures contract month is generally used to calculate the basis.

BEAR MARKET: A period of falling market prices.

BEAR SPREAD: In most commodities and financial instruments, the term refers to selling the nearby contract month, and buying the deferred contract, to profit from a change in the price relationship.

BEAR: Someone who thinks market prices will go down.

BID: An expression indicating ones desire to buy at a given price.

BOOK ENTRY SECURITIES: Electronically recorded securities that include each creditor's name, address, Social Security or tax identification number, and dollar amount loaned.

BROKER: A company or individual that executes futures, options or securities orders on behalf of financial and commercial institutions and/or the general public.

BROKERAGE FEE: The fee charged by a broker for executing a transaction.

BROKERAGE HOUSE: An individual or organization that solicits or accepts orders to buy or sell futures contracts or options on futures and accepts money or other assets from customers to support such orders. Also referred to as "commission house" or "wire house".

BULL MARKET: A period of ascending market prices.

BULL SPREAD: In most commodities and financial instruments, the term refers to buying the nearby month, and selling the back month, to profit from a change in the price relationship.

BULL: Someone who thinks market prices will go up.

BUTTERFLY SPREAD: The placing of two interdelivery spreads in opposite directions with the center delivery month common to both spreads.

C

CALENDAR SPREAD: The purchase of one delivery month of a given futures contract and simultaneous sale of another delivery month of the same commodity on the same exchange. The purchase of either a call or put option and the simultaneous sale of the same type of option with typically the same strike price but with a different expiration month.

CALL OPTION: An option that gives the buyer the right, but not the obligation, to purchase (go long) the underlying futures contract or security at the strike price on or before the expiration date.

CARRYING CHARGE: In interest rate futures markets, it refers to the differential between the yield on a cash instrument and the cost of funds necessary to buy the instrument. Also referred to as cost of carry or carry.

CASH SETTLEMENT: Transactions generally involving index-based futures contracts that are settled in cash based on the actual value of the index on the last trading day, in contrast to those that specify the delivery of a commodity or financial instrument or security.

CERTIFICATE OF DEPOSIT (CD): A time deposit with a specific maturity evidenced by a certificate.

CHARTING: Graphical depiction of past price movements in a security or commodity. Those who use charting as an analytical method plot such factors as high, low, and settlement prices, average price movements, volume, and open interest. Basic types of price charts include bar charts, point-and-figure charts, candlestick charts, and line charts. Used to anticipate future price movement using historical prices, trading volume, open interest and other trading data. Patterns formed by charting past price movements tend to repeat themselves again and again.

CLEAR: The process by which a clearinghouse maintains records of all trades and settles margin flow on a daily mark-to-market basis for its clearing member.

CLASS OF OPTIONS: Option contracts of the same type (call or put) and Style (American, European or Capped) that cover the same underlying security.

CLEARING MEMBER: A member of an exchange clearinghouse. Memberships in clearing organizations are usually held by companies. Clearing members are responsible for the financial commitments of customers that clear through their firm.

CLEARINGHOUSE: An agency or separate corporation of a futures exchange that is responsible for settling trading accounts, clearing trades, collecting and maintaining margin monies, regulating delivery, and reporting trading data. Clearinghouses act as third parties to all futures and options contracts–acting as a buyer to every clearing member seller and a seller to every clearing member buyer.

CLOSING PRICE: The last price paid for a future, option or security on any trading day. The exchange clearinghouse determines a firm's net gains or losses, margin requirements, and the next day's price limits, based on settlement prices. If there is a closing range of prices, the settlement price is determined by averaging those prices. Also referred to as settlement price.

CLOSING RANGE: The range of prices at which buy and sell transactions took place during the market close.

COMMISSION HOUSE: An individual or organization that solicits or accepts orders to buy or sell futures contracts or options on futures and accepts money or other assets from customers to support such orders. Also referred to as "wire house'.

COMMODITY FUTURES TRADING COMMISSION (CFTC): A federal regulatory agency established under the Commodity Futures Trading Commission Act, that oversees futures trading in the United States. The commission is comprised of five commissioners, one of which is designated as chairman, all of which are appointed by the President subject to Senate confirmation. The CFTC is independent of all cabinet departments.

COMMODITY POOL OPERATOR: An individual or organization that operates or solicits funds for a commodity pool.

COMMODITY POOL: An enterprise in which funds contributed by a number of persons are combined for the purpose of trading futures contracts or commodity options.

COMMODITY TRADING ADVISOR: A person who, for compensation or profit, directly or indirectly advises others on futures trading matters. Advising indirectly includes exercising trading authority over customers' accounts as well as providing recommendations through written publications or other media.

COMMON STOCK: Securities representing ownership interest in a public corporation. Owners are entitled to vote on the selection of directors and other important matters as well as to receive dividends when they are declared. If a corporation is liquidated, the claims of secured and unsecured creditors, bondholders and owners of preferred stock have priority over the claims of common stockholders.

CONCURRENT INDICATORS: Market indicators showing the general direction of the economy and confirming or denying the trend implied by the leading indicators.

CONSUMER PRICE INDEX (CPI): A major inflation measure computed by the U.S. Department of Commerce. It measures the change in prices of a fixed basket of goods and services in the previous month.

CONTRACT MONTH: A specific month in which delivery may take place under the terms of a futures contract.

CONTROLLED ACCOUNT: An arrangement by which the holder of the account gives written power of attorney to another person, often his broker, to make trading decisions. Also called a discretionary or managed account.

CONVERGENCE: The word used for referring to cash and futures prices tending to come together (i.e., the basis approaches zero) as the futures contract nears expiration.

COST OF CARRY (OR CARRY): For physical commodities such as grains and metals, the cost of storage space, insurance, and finance charges incurred by holding a physical commodity. In interest rate futures markets, it refers to the differential between the yield on a cash instrument and the cost of funds necessary to buy the instrument.

CUSTOMER MARGIN: Within the futures industry, financial guarantees required of both buyers and sellers of futures contracts and sellers of options contracts to ensure fulfilling of contract obligations. FCMs are responsible for overseeing customer margin accounts. Margins are determined on the basis of market risk and contract value. Also referred to as performance-bond margin. Financial safeguards to ensure that clearing members (usually companies or corporations) perform on their customers' open futures and options contracts. Clearing margins are distinct from customer margins that individual buyers and sellers of futures and options contracts are required to deposit with brokers.

D

DAY TRADERS: Speculators who take positions in futures or options contracts or securities and liquidate them prior to the close of the same trading day.

DEFERRED (DELIVERY) MONTH: The more distant month(s) in which futures trading is taking place, as compared from the nearby (delivery) month.

DELIVERY MONTH: A specific month in which delivery may take place under the terms of a futures contract. Also referred to as contract month.

DELIVERY: The transfer of the cash commodity from the seller of a futures contract to the buyer of a futures contract. Each futures exchange has specific procedures for delivery of a cash commodity. Some futures contracts, such as stock index contracts, are cash settled.

DELTA: A measure of how much an option premium changes, given a unit change in the underlying futures price. Delta often is interpreted as the probability that the option will be in the money by expiration.

DERIVATIVE SECURITY: A financial security whose value is determined in part from the value and characteristics of another underlying security.

DISCOUNT METHOD: A method of paying interest by issuing a security at less than par and repaying par value at maturity. The difference between the higher par value and the lower purchase price is the interest.

DISCOUNT RATE: The interest rate charged on loans to member banks by the Federal Reserve Bank.

DISCRETIONARY ACCOUNT: An arrangement by which the holder of the account gives written power of attorney to another person, often his broker, to make trading decisions. Also known as a controlled or managed account.

E

EARNINGS: The amount of profit a corporation receives after expenses, interest, and taxes are paid.

ECONOMETRICS: The application of statistical and mathematical methods in the field of economics to test and quantify economic theories and applied to the solutions to economic problems.

EQUITY OPTIONS: Options on shares of an individual common stock.

EURODOLLARS: U.S. dollars on deposit with a bank outside of the United States and, consequently, outside the jurisdiction of the United States. The bank could be either a foreign bank or a subsidiary of a U.S. bank.

EUROPEAN-STYLE OPTIONS: An option contract that may be exercised only during a specified period of time just prior to expiration.

EXERCISE PRICE: The price at which the futures contract underlying a call or put option can be purchased (if a call) or sold (if a put). Also referred to as strike price.

EXERCISE: The action taken by the holder of a call option if he wishes to purchase the underlying futures contract or by the holder of a put option if he wishes to sell the underlying futures contract.

EXTRINSIC VALUE: The amount of money option buyers are willing to pay for an option in the anticipation that, over time, a change in the underlying futures price will cause the option to increase in value. In general, an option premium is the sum of time value and intrinsic value. Any amount by which an option premium exceeds the option's intrinsic value can be considered time value.

F

FAIR VALUE: Fair value is the theoretical assumption of where a futures contract should be priced given such things as the current index level, index dividends, days to expiration and interest rates. The actual futures price will not necessarily trade at the theoretical price, as short term supply and demand will cause price to fluctuate around fair value. Price discrepancies above or below fair value often cause arbitrageurs to return the market closer to its fair value.

FEDERAL FUNDS RATE: The interest rate charged for the use of Federal Funds.

FEDERAL FUNDS: Member bank deposits at the Federal Reserve; these funds are loaned by member banks to other member banks.

FEDERAL RESERVE SYSTEM: A central banking system in the United States, created by the Federal Reserve Act in 1913, designed to assist the nation in attaining its economic and financial goals. The structure of the Federal Reserve System includes a Board of Governors, the Federal Open Market Committee, and 12 Federal Reserve Banks.

FINANCIAL INSTRUMENT: There are two basic types: (1) a debt instrument, which is a loan with an agreement to pay back funds with interest; (2) an equity security, which is share or stock in a company.

FLOOR BROKER: An individual who executes orders for the purchase or sale of any commodity futures or options contract on any contract market for any other person.

FLOOR TRADER: An individual who executes trades for the purchase or sale of any commodity futures or options contract on any contract market for their own account.

FOREIGN EXCHANGE MARKET: An over-the-counter market where buyers and sellers conduct foreign exchange business by telephone or electronically. Also referred to as a forex market.

FORWARD (CASH) CONTRACT: A cash contract in which a seller agrees to deliver a specific cash commodity to a buyer sometime in the future. Forward contracts, in contrast to futures contracts, are privately negotiated and are not standardized.

FUNDAMENTAL ANALYSIS: A method of anticipating future price movement using supply and demand information.

FUTURES COMMISSION MERCHANT (FCM): An organization that solicits or accepts orders to buy or sell futures contracts or options on futures and accepts money or other assets from customers to support such orders. Also referred to as "commission house" or "wire house."

FUTURES CONTRACT: A standardized agreement, traded on a futures exchange, to buy or sell a commodity at a specified price at a date in the future. Specifies the commodity, quality, quantity, delivery date and delivery point or cash settlement.

FUTURES EXCHANGE: A central marketplace with established rules and regulations where buyers and sellers meet to trade futures and options on futures contracts.

FUTURES OPTION: The option, when exercised or settled, relates to a futures contract.

FUNGIBILITY: The ability to offset and deliver like contracts traded on different exchanges.

G

GLOBEX®: A global electronic trading system offered by the Chicago Mercantile Exchange.

GAMMA: A measurement of how fast delta changes, given a unit change in the underlying futures price.

GROSS DOMESTIC PRODUCT: The value of all final goods and services produced by an economy over a particular time period, normally a year.

GROSS NATIONAL PRODUCT: Gross Domestic Product plus the income accruing to domestic residents as a result of investments abroad less income earned in domestic markets accruing to foreigners abroad.

H

HEDGER: An individual or company owning or planning to own a cash commodity–corn, soybeans, wheat, U.S. Treasury bonds, notes, bills, securites–and concerned that the cost of the commodity may change before either buying or selling it in the cash market. A hedger achieves protection against changing cash prices by purchasing (selling) futures contracts of the same or similar commodity and later offsetting that position by selling (purchasing) futures contracts of the same quantity and type as the initial transaction.

HEDGING: The practice of offsetting the price risk inherent in any cash market position by taking an equal but opposite position in the futures market. Hedgers use the futures markets to protect their business from adverse price changes. **Selling (Short) Hedge** - Selling futures contracts to protect against possible declining prices of commodities that will be sold in the future. At the time the cash commodities are sold, the open futures position is closed by purchasing an equal number and type of futures contracts as those that were initially sold. **Purchasing (Long) Hedge** - Buyer futures contracts to protect against a possible price increase of cash commodities that will be purchased in the future. At the time the cash commodities are bought, the open futures position is closed by selling an equal number and type of futures contracts as those that were initially purchased. Can be referred to as a buying hedge.

HOLDER: The purchaser of either a call or put option. Option buyers receive the right, but not the obligation, to assume a futures position. Referred to as the Option Buyer.

HORIZONTAL SPREAD: The purchase of either a call or put option and the simultaneous sale of the same type of option with typically the same strike price but with a different expiration month. Also referred to as a calendar spread.

I

IN-THE-MONEY OPTION: An option having intrinsic value. A call option is in the money if its strike price is below the current price of the underlying futures contract. A put option is in the money if its strike price is above the current price of the underlying futures contract.

INITIAL MARGIN: The amount a futures market participant must deposit into his margin account at the time he places an order to buy or sell a futures contract.

INTERDELIVERY SPREAD: The purchase of one delivery month of a given futures contract and simultaneous sale of another delivery month of the same commodity on the same exchange. Also referred to as an intramarket or calendar spread.

INTERMARKET SPREAD: The sale of a given delivery month of a futures contract on one exchange and the simultaneous purchase of the same delivery month and futures contract on another exchange.

INTRINSIC VALUE: The amount by which an option is in the money. A call option is in the money if its strike price is beneath the current price of the underlying futures contract. A put option is in the money if its strike price is above the current price of the underlying futures contract.

INTRODUCING BROKER: A person or organization that solicits or accepts orders to buy or sell futures contracts or commodity options but does not accept money or other assets from customers to support such orders.

INVISIBLE SUPPLY: Uncounted stocks of a commodity in the hands of wholesalers, manufacturers, and producers that cannot be identified accurately; stocks outside commercial channels but theoretically available to the market.

L

LAGGING INDICATORS: Market indicators showing the general direction of the economy and confirming or denying the trend implied by the leading indicators.

LAST TRADING DAY: The final day when trading may occur in a given futures or option contract month. Futures contracts outstanding at the end of the last trading day must be settled by delivery of the underlying commodity or securities or by agreement for monetary settlement.

LEADING INDICATORS: Market indicators that signal the state of the economy for the coming months. Some of the leading indicators include: average manufacturing work-week, initial claims for unemployment insurance, orders for consumer goods and material, percentage of companies reporting slower deliveries, change in manufacturers' unfilled orders for durable goods, plant and equipment orders, new building permits, index of consumer expectations, change in material prices, prices of stocks, change in money supply and others.

LEVERAGE: The ability to control large dollar amounts of a commodity or security with a comparatively small amount of capital.

LINKAGE: The ability to buy (sell) contracts on one exchange (such as the Chicago Mercantile Exchange) and later sell (buy) them on another exchange (such as the Singapore International Monetary Exchange.)

LIQUID: A characteristic of a security or commodity market with enough units outstanding to allow large transactions without a substantial change in price. Institutional investors are inclined to seek out liquid investments so that their trading activity will not influence the market price.

LIQUIDATE: Selling (or purchasing) futures contracts of the same delivery month purchased (or sold) during an earlier transaction or making (or taking) delivery of the cash commodity represented by the futures contract. Taking a second futures or options position opposite to the initial or opening position.

LONG HEDGE: Buying futures contracts to protect against a possible price increase of cash commodities that will be purchased in the future. At the time the cash commodities are bought, the open futures position is closed by selling an equal number and type of futures contracts as those that were initially purchased. Also referred to as a buying hedge.

LONG: One who has bought futures contracts or owns a cash commodity.

LOW: The lowest price of the day for a security, futures contract, option, or other traded instrument.

M

Maintenance: A set minimum margin (per outstanding futures contract) that a customer must maintain in his margin account.

Managed Futures: Represents an industry comprised of professional money mangers known as commodity trading advisors who manage client assets on a discretionary basis, using global futures markets as an investment medium.

Margin Call: A call from a clearinghouse to a clearing member, or from a brokerage firm to a customer, to bring margin deposits up to a required minimum level.

Margin: Financial safeguards to ensure that clearing members (usually companies or corporations) perform on their customers' open futures and options contracts. Clearing margins are distinct from customer margins that individual buyers and sellers of futures and options contracts or securities are required to deposit with brokers. Within the futures industry, financial guarantees required of both buyers and sellers of futures contracts and sellers of options contracts to ensure fulfilling of contract obligations. FCMs are responsible for overseeing customer margin accounts. Margins are determined on the basis of market risk and contract value. Also referred to as performance-bond margin.

Market Order: An order to buy or sell a futures contract of a given delivery month to be filled at the best possible price and as soon as possible.

Marking-to-Market: To debit or credit, trading profits or losses, on a daily basis a margin account based on the close of that day's trading session.

Minimum Price Fluctuation: The smallest allowable increment of price movement for a contract.

Money Supply: The amount of money in the economy, consisting primarily of currency in circulation plus deposits in banks: M-1–U.S. money supply consisting of currency held by the public, traveler's checks, checking account funds, NOW and super- NOW accounts, automatic transfer service accounts, and balances in credit unions. M-2–U.S. money supply consisting M-1 plus savings and small time deposits (less than $100,000) at depository institutions, overnight repurchase agreements at commercial banks, and money market mutual fund accounts. M-3–U.S. money supply consisting of M-2 plus large time deposits ($100,000 or more) at depository institutions, repurchase agreements with maturities longer than one day at commercial banks, and institutional money market accounts.

MOVING-AVERAGE CHARTS: The statistical price analysis method of recognizing different price trends. A moving average is calculated by adding the prices for a predetermined number of days and then dividing by the number of days.

N

NATIONAL FUTURES ASSOCIATION (NFA): An industry wide, industry-supported, self-regulatory organization for futures and options markets. The primary responsibilities of the NFA are enforcement of ethical standards, protection of customer rights, screen futures professionals for membership, audit and monitor professionals for financial and general compliance rules and provide for arbitration of futures-related disputes.

NEARBY (DELIVERY) MONTH: The futures contract month closest to expiration. Also referred to as spot month.

NEGATIVE YIELD CURVE: A chart in which the yield of debt instruments is plotted on the vertical axis and the term to maturity is plotted on the horizontal axis. The yield curve is positive when long-term rates are higher than short-term rates.

O

OFFER: An expression indicating one's desire to sell a commodity at a given price; opposite of bid.

OFFSET: Taking a second futures or options position opposite to the initial or opening position. Selling (or purchasing) futures contracts of the same delivery month purchased (or sold) during an earlier transaction or making (or taking) delivery of the cash commodity represented by the futures contract.

OPEN INTEREST: The total number of futures or options contracts of a given commodity that have not yet been offset by an opposite futures or option transaction nor fulfilled by delivery of the commodity or option exercise. Each open transaction has a buyer and a seller, but for calculation of open interest, only one side of the contract is counted.

OPEN MARKET OPERATION: The buying and selling of government securities–Treasury bills, notes, and bonds—by the Federal Reserve.

OPEN OUTCRY: Method of public auction for making verbal bids and offers in the trading pits or rings of futures exchanges.

OPENING RANGE: A range of prices at which buy and sell orders took place during the opening of the market.

OPTION BUYER: The purchaser of either a call or put option. Option buyers receive the right, but not the obligation, to assume a future or securities position. Also referred to as the holder.

OPTION PREMIUM: The sum of money that the option buyer pays and the option seller receives for the rights granted by the option.

OPTION SELLER: The person who sells an option in return for a premium and is obligated to perform when the holder exercises his right under the option contract. Also referred to as the writer.

OPTION SPREAD: The simultaneous purchase and sale of one or more options contracts, futures, and/or cash positions.

OPTION WRITER: The person who sells an option in return for a premium and is obligated to perform when the holder exercises his right under the option contract. Also referred to as the Option Seller.

OPTION: A contract that conveys the right, but not the obligation, to buy or sell a particular item at a certain price for a limited time. Only the seller of the option is obligated to perform.

OUT-OF-THE-MONEY OPTION: An option with no intrinsic value, i.e., a call whose strike price is considerably above the current futures price or a put whose strike price is below the current futures price.

OVER-THE-COUNTER MARKET: A market where products such as stocks, foreign currencies, and other cash items are bought and sold by telephone and other means of communications. (An off exchange transaction).

P

PAR: The face value of a security. For example, a bond selling at par is worth the same dollar amount it was issued for or at which it will be redeemed at maturity.

P/E RATIO: The relationship between a stock's price and its earnings per share. It is calculated by dividing the stock's price per share by earnings per share for a twelve month period. For instance, a stock selling for $25 a share and earning $5 a share is said to be selling at a P/E ratio of 5. The ratio, also known as the "multiple," gives an investor an approximation of how much they are paying for a corporation's earning power. Low P/E stocks are usually in mature industries. They may be blue chip or out of favor companies. In either case, their growth potential is limited. Companies with high P/E ratios (over 20) are usually up-and-comers that are fast growing.

PERFORMANCE BOND (MARGIN): The amount of money deposited by both buyers and sellers of futures contracts or options sellers to ensure performance of the terms of the contract. Margin in futures is not a down payment on the contract itself, but rather a security deposit. Within the futures industry, financial guarantees are required of both buyers and sellers of futures contracts and sellers of options contracts to ensure fulfillment of contract obligations. FCMs are responsible for overseeing customer margin accounts. Margins are determined on the basis of market risk and contract value. Margins are financial safeguards to ensure that clearing members (usually companies or corporations) perform on their customers' open futures and options contracts. Clearing margins are distinct from customer margins that individual buyers and sellers of futures and options contracts are required to deposit with brokers.

PIT: The area on the trading floor where futures and options on futures contracts are bought and sold. Pits are usually raised octagonal platforms with steps descending on the inside that permit buyers and sellers to see each other.

POSITION LIMIT: Maximum number of speculative futures contracts one can hold as determined by the Commodity Futures Trading Commission and/or the exchange upon which the contract is traded. Also referred to as trading limit.

POSITION: A buyer of a futures contract is said to have a long position and, conversely, a seller of futures contracts is said to have a short position.

PREFERRED STOCK: A preferred stock is a type of capital stock that pays dividends at a set rate (at the time of issuance). Dividend payments to preferred holders must be made before common stock dividends can be paid. Preferred stocks usually do not have voting rights.

PREMIUM: (1) The additional payment allowed by exchange regulation for delivery of higher-than-required standards or grades of a commodity against a futures contract. (2) In speaking of price relationships between different delivery months of a given commodity, one is said to be "trading at a premium" over another when its price is greater than that of the other. (3) In financial instruments, the dollar amount by which a security trades above its principal value. (4) The price of an option–the sum of money that the option buyer pays and the option seller receives for the rights granted by the option.

PRICE DISCOVERY: The generation of information about "future" cash market prices through the futures markets.

PRICE LIMIT: The maximum advance or decline–from the previous day's settlement–permitted for a contract in one trading session by the rules of the exchange.

PRIMARY DEALER: A designation given by the Federal Reserve System to commercial banks or broker/dealers who meet specific criteria. Among the criteria are capital requirements and meaningful participation in the Treasury auctions.

PRIME RATE: The interest rate charged by major banks to their most creditworthy customers.

PRODUCER PRICE INDEX (PPI): An index that shows the cost of resources needed to produce manufactured goods during the previous month.

PURCHASE AND SELL STATEMENT (P&S): A Statement sent by a commission house to a customer when his futures or options on futures position has changed, showing the number of contracts bought or sold, the prices at which the contracts were bought or sold, the gross profit or loss, the commission charges, and the net profit or loss on the transaction.

PURCHASING HEDGE OR LONG HEDGE: Purchase of futures contracts to protect against a possible price increase of cash commodities that will be purchased in the future. At the time the cash commodities are bought, the open futures position is closed by selling an equal number and type of futures contracts as those that were initially purchased. Also referred to as a buying hedge. The practice of offsetting the price risk inherent in any cash market position by taking an equal but opposite position in the futures market. Hedgers use the futures markets to protect their business from adverse price changes.

PUT OPTION: An option that gives the option buyer the right but not the obligation to sell (go "short") the underlying futures contract at the strike price on or before the expiration date.

R

RANGE (PRICE): The price span during a given trading session, week, month, year, etc.

REPURCHASE AGREEMENTS OR (REPO): An agreement between a seller and a buyer, usually in U.S. government securities, in which the seller agrees to buy back the security at a later date.

RESISTANCE: A level above which prices have had trouble penetrating.

S

SECONDARY MARKET: Market where previously issued securities are bought and sold.

SECURITY: Common or preferred stock; a bond of a corporation, government, or quasi-government body.

SELLING HEDGE OR SHORT HEDGE: (1) Sale of futures contracts to protect against possible declining prices of commodities that will be sold in the future. At the time the cash commodities are sold the open futures position is closed out by purchasing an equal number and type of futures contracts as those that were initially sold. (2) The practice of offsetting the price risk inherent in any cash market position by taking an equal but opposite position in the futures market. Hedgers use the futures markets to protect their business from adverse price changes.

SELLING SHORT SECURITIES: The sale of a security that the investor does not own in order to take advantage of an anticipated decline in the price of the security. In order to sell short, the investor must borrow the security from his broker to make delivery to the buyer. The short seller will eventually have to buy the security back, or buy to cover, in order to return it to the broker. Short sales are regulated by Regulation T of the Federal Reserve Board.

SETTLE: The last price paid for a commodity on any trading day. The exchange clearinghouse determines a firm's net gains or losses, margin requirements, and the next day's price limits, based on each futures and options contract settlement price. If there is a closing range of prices, the settlement price is determined by averaging those prices. Also referred to as settlement price or closing price.

SHORT HEDGE: Selling futures contracts to protect against possible declining prices of commodities that will be sold in the future. At the time the cash commodities are sold, the open futures position is closed by purchasing an equal number and type of futures contracts as those that were initially sold.

SPOT MONTH: That futures contract month closest to expiration. Also referred to as nearby delivery month.

SPOT: Usually refers to a cash market price for a physical commodity that is available for immediate delivery.

SPREAD: The price difference between two related markets or commodities.

SPREADING: The simultaneous buying and selling of two related markets in the expectation that a profit will be made when the position is offset. Examples include: buying one futures contract and selling another futures contract of the same commodity or single stock futures contract but different delivery month; buying and selling the same delivery month of the same commodity on different futures exchanges; buying a given delivery month of one futures market and selling the same delivery month of a different, but related, futures market.

STOCK DIVIDEND: A dividend that is paid in securities, rather than cash. The additional shares may be of the issuing company, or of a subsidiary.

STOCKHOLDER: An individual who owns one or more shares of a corporation's stock, whether common or preferred stock. Stockholders may earn dividends and stockholders who have common stock have voting rights with regard to matters that affect the corporation.

STOCK INDEX: An indicator that is used to measure and report value changes in a selected group of stocks. Can be in the same industry. How a particular stock index tracks the market depends on its composition–the sampling of stocks, the weighing of individual stocks, and the method of averaging used to establish an index.

STOCK MARKET: A market in which shares of stock are bought and sold.

STOCK SPLIT: Partitioning the outstanding shares of a corporation into a larger number of shares, without affecting shareholders' equity or the total market value at the time of the split. For instance, if a stock valued at $100 splits 2-for-1, an investor who owns 100 shares would now own 200 shares valued at $50. Splits usually must be voted on by directors and approved by shareholders.

STRIKE PRICE: The stated price per share for which the underlying security may be purchased (in the case of a call) or sold (in the case of a put) by the option holder upon exercise of the option contract.

SUPPORT: A price level where buying is sufficient to halt a price decline.

T

TECHNICAL ANALYSIS: Anticipating future price movement using historical prices, trading volume, open interest and other trading data to study price patterns.

TICK: The smallest allowable increment of price movement for a contract.

TIME VALUE: The amount of money option buyers are willing to pay in the anticipation that over time, a change in the underlying futures price will cause the option to increase in value. In general, an option premium is the sum of time value and intrinsic value. Any amount by which an option premium exceeds the option's intrinsic value can be considered time value. Some refer to it as extrinsic value.

TRADE BALANCE: The difference between a nation's imports and exports of merchandise.

U

UNCOVERED PUT WRITING: A short put option position in which the writer does not have a corresponding short position in the underlying security or has not deposited, in a cash account, cash or cash equivalents equal to the exercise value of the put.

UNDERLYING SECURITY: The security subject to being purchased or sold upon exercise of an option contract.

U.S. TREASURY BILL: A short-term U.S. government debt instrument with an original maturity of one year or less. Bills are sold at a discount from par with the interest earned being the difference between the face value received at maturity and the price paid.

U.S. TREASURY BOND: Government-debt security with a coupon and original maturity of more than 10 years. Interest is paid semiannually.

U.S. TREASURY NOTE: Government-debt security with a coupon and original maturity of one to 10 years.

UNDERLYING FUTURES CONTRACT: The specific futures contract that is bought or sold by exercising an option.

UPTICK: Security transaction executed at a price higher than the preceding transaction in the same security—also called a "plus tick." Short sales can only be executed on upticks or zero plus ticks.

V

VERSUS CASH: A transaction generally used by two hedgers who want to exchange futures for cash positions. Also referred to as "against actuals" or "exchange for physicals."

VERTICAL SPREAD: Buying and selling puts or calls of the same expiration month but different strike prices.

VOLATILITY: A measurement of the change in price over a given period. It is often expressed as a percentage and computed as the annualized standard deviation of the percentage change in daily price.

VOLUME: The number of purchases or sales of a share or contract made during a specific period of time, often for one trading day.

W

WIRE HOUSE: An individual or organization that solicits or accepts orders to buy or sell futures contracts or options on futures and accepts money or other assets from customers to support such orders. Also referred to as "commission house" or Futures Commission Merchant (FCM).

WRITER: The person who sells an option in return for a premium and is obligated to perform when the holder exercises his right under the option contract. Also referred to as the option seller.

Y

YIELD CURVE: A chart in which the yield level of debt instruments is plotted on the vertical axis and the term to maturity is plotted on the horizontal axis. The yield curve is positive when long-term rates are higher than short-term rates.

YIELD TO MATURITY: The rate of return an investor receives if a fixed-income security is held to maturity.

YIELD: A measure of the annual return on an investment

Z

ZERO-PLUS TICK: A price that is the same as the previous trade price, but that is higher than the price of the most recent transaction.

Internet Guide for Single Stock Futures Traders

Exchanges (Worldwide)

American Stock Exchange (AMEX)

www.amex.com

Bolsa de Mercadorias & Futuros (BM&F)
www.bmf.com.br

Bolsa Mexicana de Valores
www.bmv.com.mx

Boston Stock Exchange
www.bostonstock.com

Canadian Venture Exchange
www.cdnx.com

Central Japan Commodity Exchange
www.c-com.or.jp

Chicago Board of Trade (CBOT)
www.cbot.com

Chicago Board Options Exchange (CBOE)
www.cboe.com

Chicago Mercantile Exchange (CME)

www.cme.com

Chicago Stock Exchange (CSX)

www.chicagostockex.com

Copenhagen Stock Exchange

www.xcse.dk

Deutsche Borse Group

www.deutsche-boerse.com

EUREX

www.eurex.ch

Euronext

www.euronext.com

Helsinki Securities and Derivatives Exchange (HEX)

www.hexgroup.com

Hong Kong Futures Exchange (HKFE)

www.hkfe.com

Italian Exchange

www.borsaitalia.it

International Petroleum Exchange (IPE)

www.ipe.uk.com

Kansas City Board of Trade (KCBT)

www.kcbot.com

Korea Futures Exchange (KoFEX)

www.kofex.com

Korea Stock Exchange

www.kse.or.kr

London International Financial Futures and Options Exchange (LIFFE)

www.liffe.com

London Metal Exchange (LME)

www.lme.co.uk

London Stock Exchange

www.londonstockexchange.com

Marche a Terme International de France (MATIF)

www.matif.fr

Meff

www.meff.es

Minneapolis Grain Exchange (MGE)

www.mgex.com

Montreal Exchange (ME)

www.me.org

Naqdaq LIFFE Markets (NQLX)

www.nqlx.com

National Association of Securities Dealers (NASDAQ)

www.nasdaq.com

New York Board of Trade (formerly CSCE and NYCTN)

www.nybot.com

New York Mercantile Exchange/COMEX (NYMEX & COMEX)

www.nymex.com

New York Stock Exchange (NYSE)

www.nyse.com

Osaka Securities Exchange

www.ose.or.ip/e/

Osaka Mercantile Exchange
www.osamex.com

Oslo Stock Exchange
www.ose.no

Pacific Exchange (PCX)
www.pacificex.com

Philadelphia Stock Exchange (PHLX)
www.phlx.com

Russian Exchange (INDX)
www.re.ru

Shanghai Metal Exchange (SHME)
www.sh.com/exchange/shme/shme.htm

Singapore International Monetary Exchange Ltd (SIMEX)
www.sgx.com

South African Futures Exchange (SAFEX)
www.safex.co.za

Sydney Futures Exchange Ltd. (SFE)
www.sfe.com.au

Taiwan Futures Exchange
www.tse.com.tw

Tel Aviv Stock Exchange
www.tase.co.il

Toronto Stock Exchange (TSE)
www.tse.com

Tokyo Commodity Exchange
www.tocom.or.jp

Tokyo Grain Exchange (TGE)
www.tge.or.jp

Tokyo International Financial Futures Exchange
www.tiffe.or.jp

Tokyo Stock Exchange
www.tse.or.jp

Wiener Boerse
www.wienerboerse.at/cms

Winnipeg Commodity Exchange (WCE)
www.wce.mb.ca

Organizations and Regulatory Agencies (U.S.)

Commodity Futures Trading Commission (CFTC)

www.cftc.gov

Futures Industry Association (FIA)

www.futuresindustry.org

Global Association of Risk Professionals (GARP)

www.garp.com

Managed Funds Association (MFA)

www.mfainfo.org

Marhedge

www.marhedge.com

NASD Regulation, Inc

www.nasdr.com

National Futures Association (NFA)

www.nfa.futures.org

National Introducing Brokers Association (NIBA)

www.theniba.com

Securities and Exchange Commission (SEC)

www.sec.gov

News Services

Bloomberg Online News
www.bloomberg.com

Business Wire
www.businesswire.com

CNBC
www.cnbc.com

CNN Money
www.money.cnn.com

Financial Times
www.ft.com

Futures and Options World
www.fow.com

EDGAR Online News
www.edgar-online.com

CBS Marketwatch
www.cbsmarketwatch.com

Futures Magazine
www.futuresmag.com

MSN Money
www.moneycentral.com

Reuters
www.reuters.com

Stocks and Commodities Magazine
www.traders.com

The Street.com
www.thestreet.com

Wall Street Journal
www.wsj.com

Wall Street City
www.wallstreetcity.com

Futures World News
www.fwn.com

INO Global Markets
www.ino.com

Quotes And Charts

PC Quote
www.pcquote.com

Barchart.com
www.barchart.com

BigCharts
www.bigcharts.com

ClearStation
www.clearstation.com

DTN.IQ
www.dtniq.com

Price Charts Dot Com
www.pricecharts.com

CQG
www.cqg.com

FutureSource
www.futuresource.com

eSignal
www.esignal.com

Order Types

FUTURES

These are common order types for most futures contracts. Orders types accepted on various electronic platforms vary and you should check with your Broker-Dealer or Futures Commission Merchant for the order rules in effect at the electronic exchange where your order is placed.

ALL-OR-NONE

An order to be executed only in its entirety or not at all. An order must be designated as an ALL-OR-NONE to be executed as such.

DAY ORDER (Day Order)

Unless marked otherwise, all orders are considered good for the day orders, also known as "day orders." This type of order expires if it hasn't been executed by the close of trading on the same day it was entered. Good for the day orders entered after the market closes are valid for the following trading day only.

FOK ORDER (Fill or Kill)

Designation added to an order which instructs the broker to offer or bid one time only. If the order is not filled immediately, it is then automatically cancelled.

LIMIT ORDER

To be executed at a specific price or better.

MIT (Market If Touched)

Orders placed higher or lower in the current market. A sell (MIT) is placed above the market, and a buy (MIT) is placed below. When the designated price is touched, it becomes a market order.

MARKET ORDER

To be executed upon receipt at the best available price.

MOC ORDER (Market-On-Close)

To be executed as a market order only in the closing range.

OCO ORDER (One-Cancels-Other)

A combination of two orders, in which the execution of either one automatically cancels the other.

OPEN ORDER (Good-Till-Cancelled)

Remains in force until cancelled. Without such designation, all unfilled orders are cancelled at the end of the trading session.

OPENING ONLY ORDER

An order that is to be executed in the initial regular trading hours (RTH) session opening range. Any such order or portion thereof not so executed shall be treated and reported as "unable" to the customer within a reasonable time.

SPREAD ORDER

A combination of buy and sell orders in different contract months within one commodity, or between two different commodities (mixed spread), at the market or at a fixed differential.

STOP ORDER

An order which becomes a market order when the price designated on the order (the "Stop" price) is elected as described below.

A "Buy Stop" order is placed at a price above the market. It is elected only when the market trades at or above, or is bid at or above the stop price.

A "Sell Stop" order is placed at a price below the market. It is elected only when the market trades at or below, or is offered at or below, the stop price.

STOP-CLOSE-ONLY ORDER

A stop order which is in effect only during the closing range. It becomes a market order if, during the closing range, the market:

(1) in the case of a buy-stop-close order, trades at or above, or is bid at or above the stop price; or (2) in the case of a sell-stop-close only order, trades at or below, or is offered at or below the stop price.

Bibliography

Security Analysis by Benjamin Graham, David L. Dodd

Book Description

This classic book secured Benjamin Graham's immortality on Wall Street. The carefully honed methods for finding undervalued stocks and bonds he described here have never been equaled, and have already outlived their author by more than 20 years. Even though this book has gone through five editions and nearly a million copies, you can learn time-tested investment secrets and strategies by going back to the source—THE ORIGINAL—and paying close attention to its wisdom. Written just five years after the crash, the message today is just as vivid, just as lucid, and just as vital as it was in 1934.

Option Volatility & Pricing: Advanced Trading Strategies and Techniques by Sheldon Natenberg

Book Description

One of the most widely read books among active option traders around the world, this book has been completely updated to reflect the most current developments and trends in option products and trading strategies.

Written in a clear, easy-to-understand fashion, it points out the key concepts essential to succeeding in trading. Drawing on his experience as a professional trader, author Sheldon Natenberg examines both the theory and reality of option trading. He presents the foundations of option theory explaining how this theory can be used to identify and exploit trading opportunities. *Option Volatility & Pricing* teaches you to use a wide variety of trading strategies and shows you how to select the strategy that best fits your view of market conditions and individual risk tolerance.

Technical Analysis of the Financial Markets : A Comprehensive Guide to Trading Methods and Applications by John J. Murphy

Book Description

This outstanding reference has taught thousands of traders the concepts of technical analysis and its application in futures and stock markets. Covering the latest developments in computer technology, technical tools, and indicators, the second edition features new material on candlestick charting, intermarket relationships, stocks and stock rotation, plus state-of-the-art examples and figures. From how to read charts to understanding indicators and the crucial role technical analysis plays in investing, readers gain a thorough and accessible overview of the field of technical analysis, with a special emphasis on futures markets. Revised and expanded for the demands of today's financial world, this book is essential reading for anyone interested in tracking and analyzing market behavior.

Futures: Fundamental Analysis by Jack D. Schwager, Steven C. Turner

Book Description

In *Fundamental Analysis*, Jack Schwager has produced the most comprehensive, in-depth book ever written on the use of fundamental analysis for futures trading. In what is destined to become the bible of the futures industry, Schwager shares insights gathered during his long career as a trader, researcher, best selling writer, and highly regarded authority in the field.

Trading S&P Futures and Options by Humphrey Lloyd

Book Description

An introduction to trading in S&P 500 futures, e-mini futures, and index option markets. Provides an overview of man momentum and other technical indicators that maybe employed for intermediate and short term market timing. Chart patterns are described and classified as favorable and unfavorable. Certain combinations of indicators are shown which may offer effective trading signals. Discusses the types of orders that may be employed in trading futures and options contracts and how to place such orders. This is an excellent book for new traders. Available direct from the publisher at a 40% discount from $49 price by calling 800-927-8222.

The Disciplined Trader: Developing Winning Attitudes by Mark Douglas

Book Description

With rare insight based on his first-hand commodity trading experience, Mark Douglas demonstrates why the beliefs learned to function effectively in society are often formidable psychological barriers in trading. *The Disciplined Trader* helps you join the elite few who have learned how to control their trading behavior by developing a systematic, step-by-step approach for winning — week after week, month after month.

In a comprehensive and logical manner, Mark Douglas shows you how to examine and limit your trading behavior — how to develop the mental discipline possessed by the small minority of winners who make money consistently

Trading for a Living: Psychology, Trading Tactics, and Money Management by Alexander Elder

Book Description

An eminent futures trader explores crucial factors that most experts overlook—time, volume and open interest—and describes little-known indicators to profitably track them. Covers all the popular technical approaches to futures, options and equities including Elliott Wave, oscillators, moving averages, market logic, point-and-figure charting. He also explains why most traders sabotage themselves and how to avoid doing the same

All of these books are many others are available through:

Traders Press, Inc.
P.O. Box 6206
Greenville SC 29606
800-927-8222 ~ 864-298-0222 ~ Fax 864-298-0221
www.traderspress.com   tradersprs@aol.com.

Contact them for a free copy of their *Traders Catalog,* which describes hundreds of books, courses, and videos of interest to traders and investors in equities, options, and futures.

FREE NEWSLETTER, UPDATES AND SPECIAL OFFERS

Single stock futures trading is just beginning and many changes will be happening almost daily.

To stay up to date on the latest developments in the fast moving world of single stock futures,

Send your request to:

info@ssfbook.com
www.ssfbook.com

ABOUT THE AUTHOR

Steven A. Greenberg is a founder and is President and CEO of Alaron Trading Corporation, a national online and full-service retail brokerage firm serving individual investors in futures and futures options markets. Since 1988, Mr. Greenberg has been a member of the Chicago Mercantile Exchange, where he has served as an independent trader and broker and has sat on various exchange committees. Mr.Greenberg is widely quoted by leading business media on a variety of derivatives industry topics and trends and he has been profiled by the *Chicago Sun Times* as a "Chicago business leader looking toward the 21st century." He holds a B.A. in International Relations from Boston University and lives in Chicago with his wife and three children.

TRADERS PRESS, INC.®
PO BOX 6206
Greenville, SC 29606

Publishers of:

A Complete Guide to Trading Profits (Paris)
A Professional Look at S&P Day Trading (Trivette)
Ask Mr. EasyLanguage (Tennis)
A Treasury of Wall Street Wisdom (Editors: Schultz & Coslow)
Beginner's Guide to Computer Assisted Trading (Alexander)
Channels and Cycles: A Tribute to J.M. Hurst (Millard)
Chart Reading for Professional Traders (Jenkins)
Commodity Spreads: Analysis, Selection and Trading Techniques (Smith)
Comparison of Twelve Technical Trading Systems (Lukac, Brorsen, & Irwin)
Complete Stock Market Trading and Forecasting Course (Jenkins)
Cyclic Analysis (J.M. Hurst)
Day Trading with Short Term Price Patterns (Crabel)
Exceptional Trading: The Mind Game (Roosevelt)
Fibonacci Ratios with Pattern Recognition (Pesavento)
Futures Spread Trading: The Complete Guide (Smith)
Geometry of Markets (Gilmore)
Geometry of Stock Market Profits (Jenkins)
Harmonic Vibrations (Pesavento)
How to Trade in Stocks (Livermore & Smitten)
Hurst Cycles Course (J.M. Hurst)
Investing by the Stars (Weingarten)
Jesse Livermore: Speculator King (Sarnoff)
Magic of Moving Averages (Lowry)
Market Rap: The Odyssey of a Still-Struggling Commodity Trader (Collins)
Pit Trading: Do You Have the Right Stuff? (Hoffman & Baccetti)
Planetary Harmonics of Speculative Markets (Pesavento)
Point & Figure Charting (Aby)
Point & Figure Charting: Commodity and Stock Trading Techniques (Zieg)
Profitable Grain Trading (Ainsworth)
Profitable Patterns for Stock Trading (Pesavento)
Short-Term Trading with Price Patterns (Harris)
Stock Market Trading Systems (Appel & Hitschler)
Stock Patterns for Day Trading (Rudd)
Stock Patterns for Day Trading 2 (Rudd)
Stock Patterns for Day Trading Home Study Course (Rudd)
Stock Trading Techniques Based on Price Patterns (Harris)
Study Helps in Point & Figure Techniques (Wheelan)
Technically Speaking (Wilkinson)
Technical Trading Systems for Commodities and Stocks (Patel)
The Amazing Life of Jesse Livermore: World's Greatest Stock Trader (Smitten)
The Opening Price Principle: The Best Kept Secret on Wall Street (Pesavento)
The Professional Commodity Trader (Kroll)
The Taylor Trading Technique (Taylor)
The Traders (Kleinfeld)
*The Trading Rule That Can Make You Rich** (Dobson)
Trading Secrets of the Inner Circle (Goodwin)
Trading S&P Futures and Options (Lloyd)
Twelve Habitudes of Highly Successful Traders (Roosevelt)
Understanding Bollinger Bands (Dobson)
Understanding Fibonacci Numbers (Dobson)
Viewpoints of a Commodity Trader (Longstreet)
Wall Street Ventures & Adventures Through Forty Years (Wyckoff)
When Supertraders Meet Kryptonite (Collins)
Winning Market Systems (Appel)

PLEASE CONTACT TRADERS PRESS TO RECEIVE OUR CURRENT CATALOG DESCRIBING THESE
AND MANY OTHER BOOKS AND GIFTS OF INTEREST TO INVESTORS AND TRADERS.
800-927-8222 ~ Fax 864-298-0221 ~ 864-298-0222
http://www.TradersPress.com~tradersprs@aol.com

Traders Press, Inc.®

Publishes books exclusively
for traders and investors.

• Publishes largest catalog collection of financial
classics in the U.S.
• Catalogs and publishes over 650 titles
for the successful trader.

Traders Press, Inc.®—order our catalog—hundreds of books,
tapes, courses and gifts of interest to all market traders
(Regular price $10)

Get a **FREE** copy by contacting
Traders Press

800-927-8222
864-298-0222
FAX 864-298-0221
tradersprs@aol.com
http://www.TradersPress.com

Traders Press, Inc.®
PO Box 6206
Greenville, SC 29606

Serving Traders Since 1975